REPAIR & RENOVATE

bathrooms

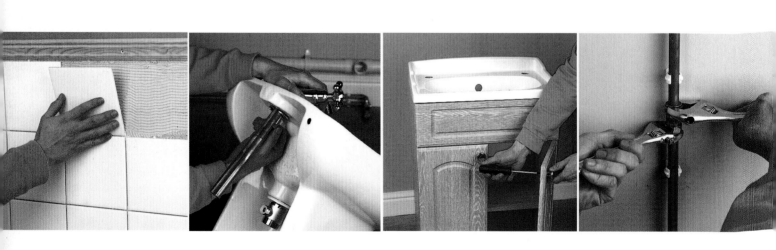

REPAIR & RENOVATE

bathrooms

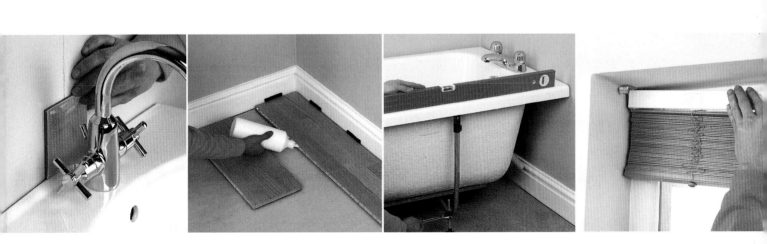

Julian Cassell & Peter Parham

MURDOCH
BOOKS

bathrooms **contents**

Installing a basin and pedestal involves rudimentary plumbing. Full instructions are given on pages 48–49.

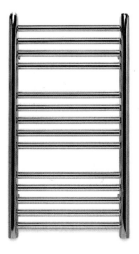

introduction

Modern lifestyles and rising standards of living mean that a bathroom is no longer a purely functional area of the home. Comfort, good looks and a relaxing atmosphere are now important considerations too. These requirements have led to huge manufacturing innovations in all areas of bathroom design ranging from the style of baths, showers and basins to smaller details such as shelves and mirrors, and even the types of specialist paint, which are now produced specifically for bathroom use.

style & design

When people think about redecorating their home, whether simply to refresh the existing style or to make a more radical design change, bathrooms are usually high on the list of target areas. This is largely because a bathroom experiences a high degree of wear and tear, and therefore, the frequency of repairs and the need for redecoration will be greater than in many other areas of the home. Whether all you plan to do is apply a new coat of paint, or you wish to make more drastic renovations such as installing a new suite, bathrooms are a popular choice for home improvement enthusiasts.

Most lifestyle magazines contain at least one article about how to improve the look of the bathroom, and they always feature plenty of photographs full of inspirational ideas. Indeed, choice has never been greater. All tastes are catered for and it is now easier than ever before to impose your personality and preferences on the look and atmosphere of your bathroom. Some of the ideas to be found in magazines are certainly more achievable – and desirable – than others, but they all provide a good point of reference when it comes to considering what it is possible to achieve and the type of work you would like to do.

BELOW *Fresh colours and natural wood panelling on the walls combine with white fixtures and chrome fittings to make the most of the natural light available in this bathroom.*

The main problem for most people when considering bathroom renovation is plumbing. They think that anything to do with plumbing is either exceptionally difficult or simply should not be attempted by non-professionals. It is certainly true that you should not take on any jobs for which you do not have the necessary knowledge or confidence. However, many tasks are in fact straightforward and it can save you a great deal of money if you do them yourself and you will ultimately feel a fine sense of achievement. Recent innovations, such as the shut-off valves that are found on most new bathroom fittings, have made many plumbing jobs much easier than in the past. These valves allow you to isolate the water supply to a single fitting, so that it is no longer necessary to shut down the entire water system of the house in order to carry out any work on a particular fitting. In addition, most large DIY outlets now supply instructions with plumbing fittings in an attempt to make more jobs possible for home improvement enthusiasts.

Before beginning any renovation project, it is important to be aware of how a bathroom actually works in terms of fittings and their supply and drainage mechanisms, as well as how the fittings are positioned to make the best use of space while still being easy to use. Chapter 1 takes

all these factors into account discussing the anatomy of bathrooms and how the various items such as basins, toilets, baths, and bidets interact. Understanding the basic principles of bathroom design is vital if you are to achieve the best possible bathroom layout.

Chapter 2 deals with the most important stage of any renovation project – the planning. The need for thorough planning is emphasized time and time again in this book, and with very good reason, since it is this stage of the job that paves the way for a successful outcome. Planning begins a long time before the first tool is picked up. Many decisions have to be made regarding the extent of work to be carried out, how much you will do yourself and whether you have the appropriate tools and materials to complete the work. The style of fittings is a matter of personal choice but always remember that you will be living with that choice for many years to come, so it is important to take time to consider all the issues very carefully before making a final decision.

ABOVE *A bathroom must be able to withstand daily use by all the family, but this need not mean style is sacrificed – here the tiled splashback is both appealingly colourful and practical.*

Chapter 3 considers the majority of bathroom fittings and the way in which they are installed. Installing a new bathroom suite is not a job that should be undertaken lightly, although you will be surprised how many tasks are more straightforward than you may at first think. If in doubt about your capabilities, always err on the side of caution. Once the main units and fittings are in place, you can then turn your attention to the various accessories that provide much of the finished look of a bathroom, and help to make it easy and comfortable to use. Chapter 4 discusses this area of renovation and points out all those details that may not be foremost in your mind when considering a bathroom revamp.

Flooring is an important issue when refurbishing a bathroom. It must be durable but also contribute to the decorative appeal of the room. Chapter 5 looks at the many flooring options and demonstrates the best techniques for achieving the desired finish. The final decorative touches to a bathroom also contribute considerably to the final look, and Chapter 6 examines this important stage.

Many of the techniques used when renovating a bathroom are similar to those employed in other parts of the home, but there are additional methods and procedures that will

help to extend the life expectancy of your bathroom finishes. However, even if you apply these techniques, all bathrooms require repairs from time to time, and this is discussed in Chapter 7. Repair jobs can range from changing washers to replacing broken tiles, all of which are important in maintaining the function and look of the room.

It is not always necessary to refit a bathroom completely in order to give it a new look. Sometimes a few simple changes are all you will need to revamp or rejuvenate the appearance of your existing bathroom. Chapter 8 provides many examples of how such alterations can improve the current look of your bathroom and provide a new appearance that will fulfil your wishes.

This book supplies a wealth of knowledge and instruction on bathroom renovation and should be of immense help in attaining your goals. Enjoy the experience of your work – the end product can be exceptionally rewarding in terms of the sense of achievement you will experience as well as the pleasure that a new bathroom design can provide.

BELOW *Watertight and easy to wipe down, tiling is the ideal decoration for wall and floor surfaces in a bathroom – a stylish effect is created here by tiling over the boxing around the bath.*

The layout of this book has been designed to give project instruction in as comprehensive yet straightforward a manner as possible. The illustration below provides a guideline to the different elements incorporated into the page design. Full colour photos and diagrams combined with explanatory text, laid out in a clear, step-by-step order, provide easy-to-follow instructions. Each project is prefaced by a blue box containing a list of tools so that you will know in advance the range of equipment required for the job. Other boxes of additional text accompany each project, which are aimed at drawing your attention to particular issues. Pink safety boxes alert the reader to issues of safety and detail any precautions that may need to be taken. They also indicate where a particular job must be carried out by a tradesperson. Green tip boxes offer professional hints for the best way to go about a particular task involved in the project. Boxes with an orange border describe alternative options and techniques, relevant to the project in hand but not demonstrated on the page.

difficulty rating

The following symbols are designed to give an indication of difficulty level relating to particular tasks and projects in this book. Clearly what are simple jobs to one person may be difficult to another, and vice versa. These guidelines are primarily based on the ability of an individual in relation to the experience and degree of technical ability required.

Straightforward and requires limited technical skills

Straightforward but requires a reasonable skill level

Technically quite difficult, and could involve a number of skills

High skill level required and involves a number of techniques

safety boxes, pink for emphasis, draw attention to safety considerations

tip boxes provide helpful hints developed from professional experience or highlight areas where more traditional methods can be used

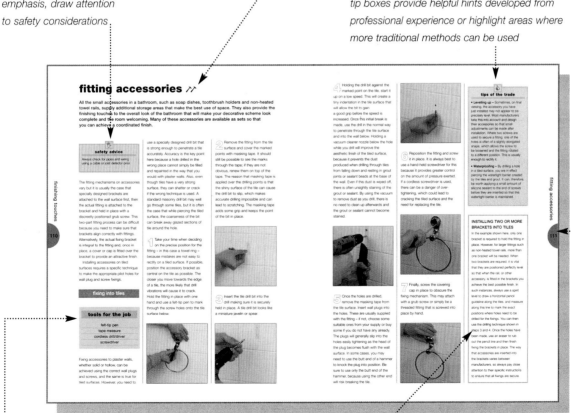

a list of tools is provided at the beginning of each job

option boxes offer additional instructions and techniques for the project in hand

colour-coordinated tabs help you find your place quickly when moving between chapters

anatomy of bathrooms

The layout of a bathroom should always offer the most practical use of space, while remaining as attractive as possible. This chapter explains the different ways in which bathrooms are designed in order to achieve these goals. Although the size of the room and the floor space available play an important part in determining the best layout, there are a number of features common to all bathrooms and about which some basic guidelines should be followed. From this initial planning point, variations can then be made to deal with personal preferences and specific needs.

When planning the bathroom design, if space is at a premium one option is to install a shower cubicle instead of a bath.

the basic shape of a bathroom

The basic shape of a bathroom is primarily affected by the size of the room and the number of items comprising a chosen suite. The number of bathrooms in a household, and thus the extent to which each bathroom is used and by how many people, will also have an influence. The bathroom is a very functional part of the home and it is important to position appliances so that they may function with optimum efficiency. The ideal area for ease of use of a particular item is referred to as 'standing room' or the 'working area', and these are demonstrated by the red boxes in the diagrams below. However, a bathroom is also a room for relaxing in, and it is important to incorporate a degree of comfort and aesthetics into the overall design.

spacious bathrooms

The larger the bathroom, the greater the choice available for design, but this still means that careful planning is essential. In fact, smaller bathrooms are often easier to design because options are limited. In general, where there is a large bathroom the available space tends to be filled with as many fittings as possible, which is satisfactory provided working areas are available for each particular fitting. Large bathrooms can be used by more than one person at the same time and it is therefore necessary for standing areas to be as separate as possible.

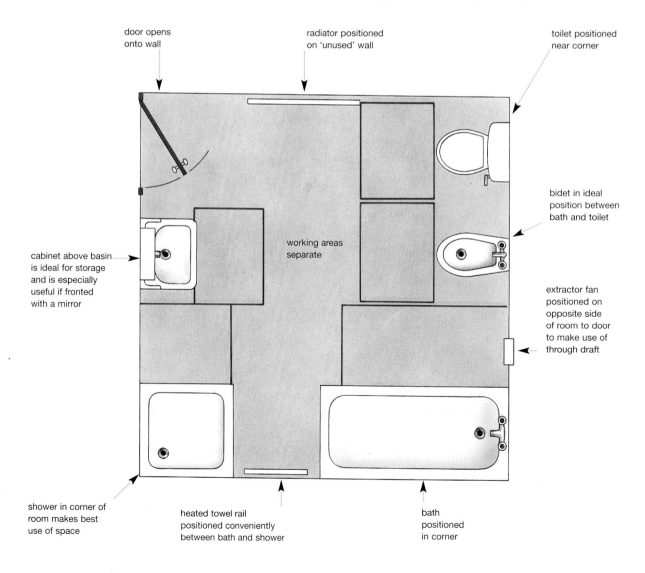

door opens onto wall

radiator positioned on 'unused' wall

toilet positioned near corner

bidet in ideal position between bath and toilet

cabinet above basin is ideal for storage and is especially useful if fronted with a mirror

working areas separate

extractor fan positioned on opposite side of room to door to make use of through draft

shower in corner of room makes best use of space

heated towel rail positioned conveniently between bath and shower

bath positioned in corner

In households with a single bathroom used by the entire family, there may need to be some compromises depending upon the available space. There are opportunities to choose fitting designs aimed at space saving, such as quadrant shower trays and a heated towel rail that also acts as the radiator in the room. Working areas may need to overlap in family bathrooms, but this can be limited to a certain extent, so that efficiency is maintained and the bathroom can still be used by more than one person at a time.

tips of the trade

Toilets should ideally be located on external walls, or close to external walls, so that the amount of plumbing required to get from the toilet to the exterior soil pipe is kept to a minimum.

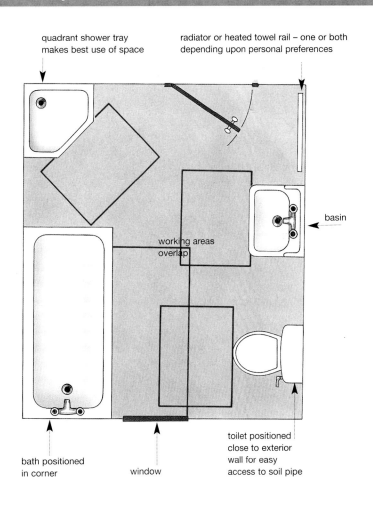

quadrant shower tray makes best use of space

radiator or heated towel rail – one or both depending upon personal preferences

basin

working areas overlap

bath positioned in corner

window

toilet positioned close to exterior wall for easy access to soil pipe

En-suite bathrooms tend to be small in size, and as such many design choices will be dictated by the space available. Since this type of bathroom is not as 'busy' as others, the idea of working or standing areas tends to become redundant. Instead, a single central space becomes the working area for all items in the bathroom. Attention is more focussed with providing easy access to the fittings in the bathroom by one person at any one time, hence the bath working area can become the basin working area depending upon which item is in use. Fitting a shower cubicle instead of a bath will allow for more space.

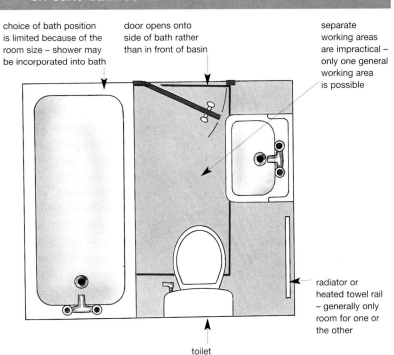

choice of bath position is limited because of the room size – shower may be incorporated into bath

door opens onto side of bath rather than in front of basin

separate working areas are impractical – only one general working area is possible

radiator or heated towel rail – generally only room for one or the other

toilet

fitted bathrooms

Clearly all bathrooms are 'fitted' in as much as the main items are permanently plumbed in and fixed in position. When the term fitted is applied to bathrooms, therefore, it usually indicates that those items are housed in specially designed units. The units usually have a collective finish and produce a continuous visual link that gives the bathroom a pleasing overall look. The term fitted is also used to indicate that pipework is boxed in and hidden from view.

bathroom units

You can build your own units if you wish or purchase custom-made versions. Manufacturers produce many different designs that can be fitted into most bathroom layouts. Although quality and price can vary dramatically, there are a number of common features in the way that units are designed and constructed. The example below shows the way in which a basin unit – sometimes called a vanity unit – is constructed.

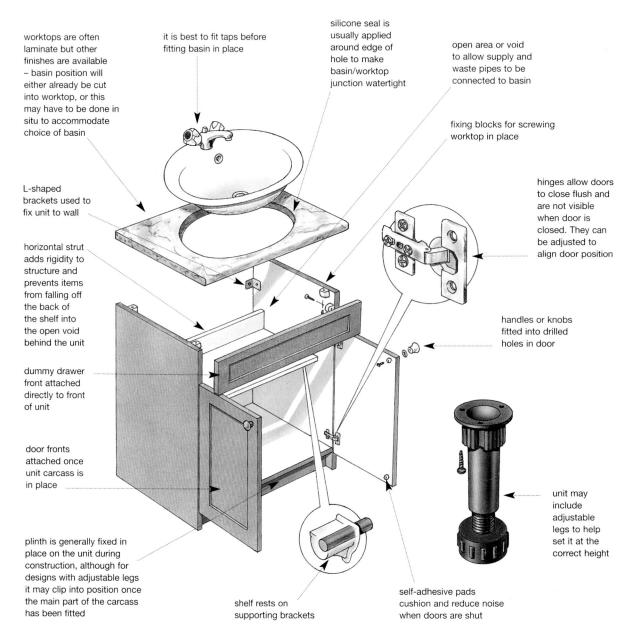

worktops are often laminate but other finishes are available – basin position will either already be cut into worktop, or this may have to be done in situ to accommodate choice of basin

it is best to fit taps before fitting basin in place

silicone seal is usually applied around edge of hole to make basin/worktop junction watertight

open area or void to allow supply and waste pipes to be connected to basin

fixing blocks for screwing worktop in place

hinges allow doors to close flush and are not visible when door is closed. They can be adjusted to align door position

L-shaped brackets used to fix unit to wall

horizontal strut adds rigidity to structure and prevents items from falling off the back of the shelf into the open void behind the unit

dummy drawer front attached directly to front of unit

door fronts attached once unit carcass is in place

handles or knobs fitted into drilled holes in door

unit may include adjustable legs to help set it at the correct height

plinth is generally fixed in place on the unit during construction, although for designs with adjustable legs it may clip into position once the main part of the carcass has been fitted

shelf rests on supporting brackets

self-adhesive pads cushion and reduce noise when doors are shut

It is possible to achieve a fitted look in one of two ways. One method is to house all the bathroom fixtures, such as the basin and toilet, within carcass units and to connect these units with extra storage and display units. Panelling can be applied around the bathtub to match the unit finish. The bath is the largest fixture in the bathroom, so panelling is an effective way of incorporating it into the decoration of the rest of the room rather than allowing it to dominate. The aim of this type of bathroom design is to hide all the pipework and connections, while maintaining maximum practicality and a modern, attractive appearance. A detailed illustration of how to achieve this look can be found on pages 18–19.

RIGHT *Unit design may be linked with other decoration in the room to enhance the fitted look. The blue colour of some of the door and drawer panels of the units in this bathroom is repeated in the colour of the walls.*

The other method for achieving a fully fitted look is to box in all unsightly elements. As well as disguising or hiding areas of pipework from view, the boxing can also be designed to provide extra shelving that is useful for both storage and display purposes. As long as the frameworks are well constructed, boxing can be just as pleasing to the eye as manufactured units. You can also apply a decorative finish to boxing frameworks, such as tiling, in order to produce a well-integrated and built-in effect. Full instructions on boxing in are given on pages 62–3.

LEFT *By decorating the boxed in areas with the same tiles used for the floor, this enhances the fitted look and gives the impression of a made-to-measure overall bathroom design.*

how fixtures & fittings are connected

The functional elements of the bathroom have to be connected to the appropriate wastes and supplies, and held securely in place with appropriate supports and fixings. Connectors, supply mechanisms and fixings can vary considerably depending on the age of the fittings and the design. However, there are certain principles that will help you to gain a better understanding of the way in which fittings are installed and positioned in order to function effectively.

baths

The size and shape of bathtubs may vary, they all require a hot and cold water supply and connection to the appropriate waste systems. The diagram below shows the mechanisms of a bath that are generally hidden from view when it is in everyday use. It is important to have a basic understanding of these before attempting to carry out any work.

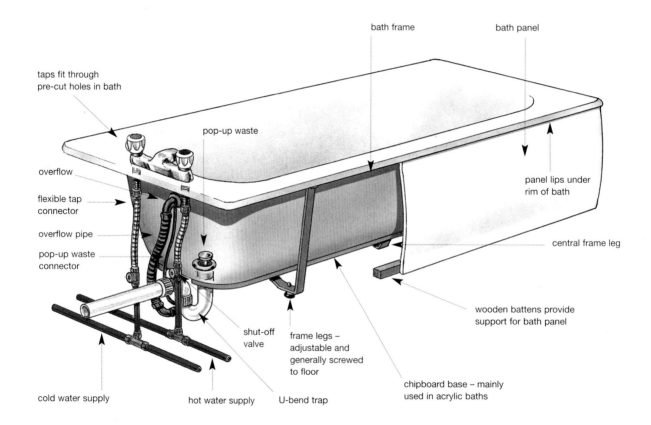

- bath frame
- bath panel
- taps fit through pre-cut holes in bath
- pop-up waste
- panel lips under rim of bath
- overflow
- flexible tap connector
- overflow pipe
- pop-up waste connector
- central frame leg
- wooden battens provide support for bath panel
- shut-off valve
- frame legs – adjustable and generally screwed to floor
- chipboard base – mainly used in acrylic baths
- cold water supply
- hot water supply
- U-bend trap

EXTRA SUPPORT

Below some bathtubs you will find extra timber, such as chipboard that is used to support the bath and distribute weight more evenly. The wood is usually hidden from view behind the bath panels.

PANELS

Bath panels are often supplied with the bathtub, but sometimes you may have to make your own. Old-fashioned roll-top baths do not require panels and usually have decorative feet that are visible at all times.

basins

Basins also vary in design but all require a water supply and waste system. Some basins are wall-mounted and some are supported by pedestals. In many fitted bathrooms, the basin is housed in a specially designed unit known as a vanity unit. The diagram on the right shows the features that are common to most sink designs and the mechanisms that allow them to function.

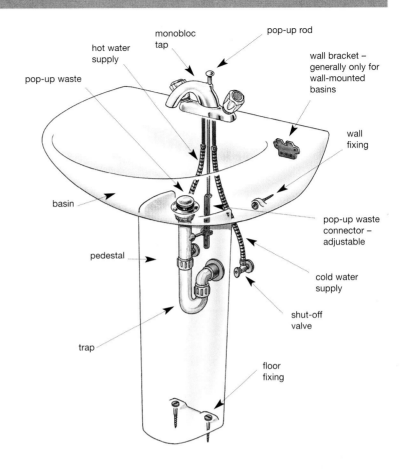

hot water supply

monobloc tap

pop-up rod

pop-up waste

wall bracket – generally only for wall-mounted basins

wall fixing

basin

pop-up waste connector – adjustable

pedestal

cold water supply

shut-off valve

trap

floor fixing

17

toilets

Toilets differ from baths and basins in that only a cold water supply is required and the waste system is of much larger proportions. The area where toilet designs can vary significantly from one another is the cistern. Traditional or more old-fashioned toilets have the cistern mounted high above the pan and are referred to as 'high level'. Another type is the 'low level' design, where the cistern is mounted on the wall just above the pan. However, most modern toilets are 'close coupled', with the cistern positioned directly on and at the back of the pan making connection much more simple. This design is demonstrated here.

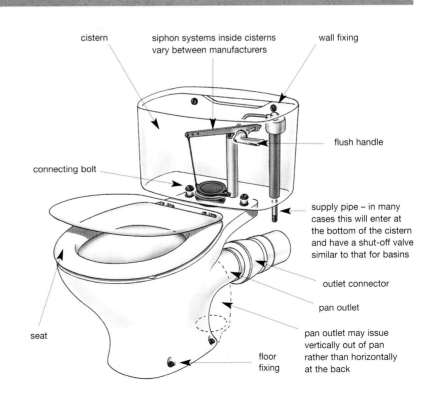

cistern

siphon systems inside cisterns vary between manufacturers

wall fixing

flush handle

connecting bolt

supply pipe – in many cases this will enter at the bottom of the cistern and have a shut-off valve similar to that for basins

outlet connector

pan outlet

seat

floor fixing

pan outlet may issue vertically out of pan rather than horizontally at the back

how bathrooms are fitted

Once you understand the basics of bathroom layout and how items are fixed in place, you need to learn how the various elements interact to become fully functional. This relationship becomes slightly more complicated when the room is fully fitted with units. The illustrations below and opposite show the relationships between fittings and how supplies are routed to them to produce the most attractive finished look for the bathroom as a whole.

units

For a fully fitted bathroom design, units are joined together to create continuous runs of units. The units at the end of a run are usually fitted with end panels at the sides (if they are visible) which match the finish of the doors. Special units are also used to house the various bathroom fixtures, such as the toilet and basin – this produces an attractive, integrated look. The diagram below identifies the various elements of a fitted bathroom and demonstrates how they are constructed.

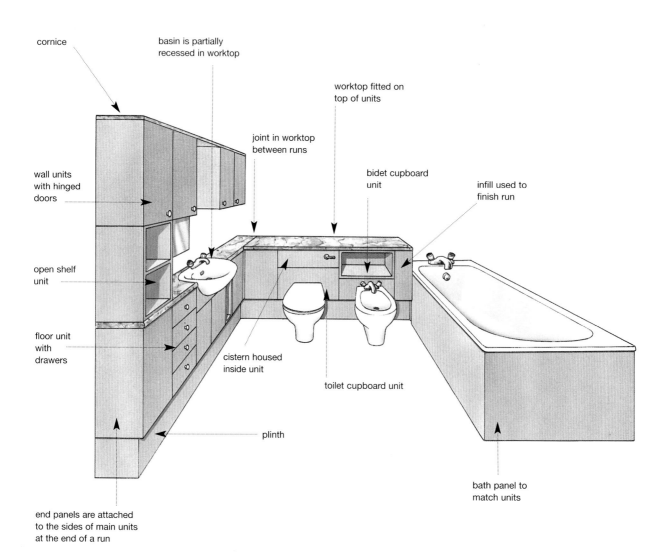

cornice

basin is partially recessed in worktop

worktop fitted on top of units

joint in worktop between runs

bidet cupboard unit

infill used to finish run

wall units with hinged doors

open shelf unit

floor unit with drawers

cistern housed inside unit

toilet cupboard unit

plinth

end panels are attached to the sides of main units at the end of a run

bath panel to match units

plumbing

The water supply and drainage requirements of a bathroom are usually more complicated than in any other room in the house, since there are likely to be more fixtures that use running water than elsewhere. Routing the necessary pipework must be planned carefully so that it can be hidden from view while still being accessible in emergencies.

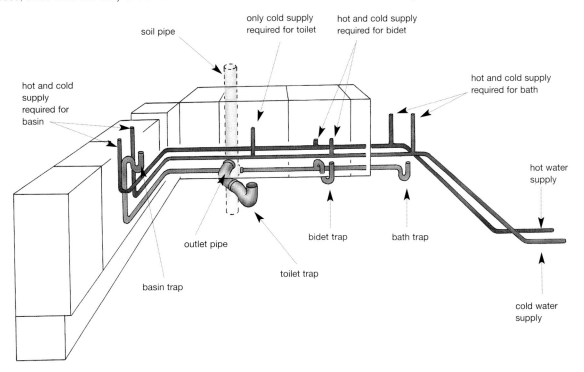

soil pipe

only cold supply required for toilet

hot and cold supply required for bidet

hot and cold supply required for bath

hot and cold supply required for basin

hot water supply

outlet pipe

bidet trap

bath trap

toilet trap

basin trap

cold water supply

electrics

Standard electrical sockets cannot be fitted in a bathroom because of the obvious danger of water coming into contact with them. However, there is still a surprising amount of wiring required in a fully functioning bathroom.

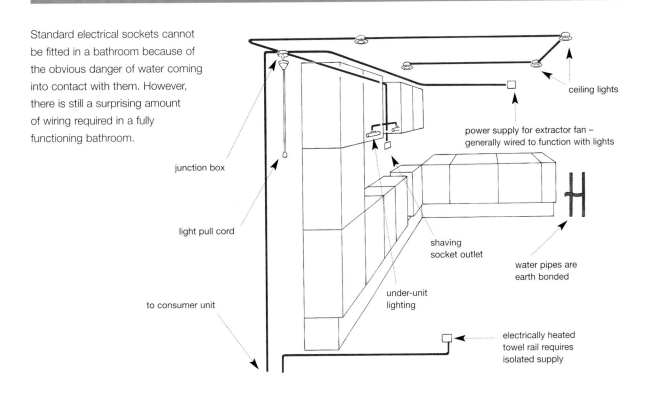

junction box

light pull cord

to consumer unit

ceiling lights

power supply for extractor fan – generally wired to function with lights

shaving socket outlet

water pipes are earth bonded

under-unit lighting

electrically heated towel rail requires isolated supply

planning

When renovating a bathroom you need to decide what changes you wish to make to the existing layout and assess the extent of work required. A complete renovation involves making a number of style choices, the most important of which will be picking a new bathroom suite or units. This chapter gives examples of various design options and outlines the main points you should consider when choosing new items. You will also need to assess how much of the work you are able to carry out yourself, both legally and according to your abilities. Once this is decided you can plan ahead for the jobs that will require a tradesperson. Guidelines are given for when it is best to seek professional help and how to plan carefully in order to achieve the best results.

The position of fixtures in this bathroom has been planned in order to fit around the large windows dominating the room.

options for change

Choosing bathroom fittings is a matter of personal preference. You need to decide whether you want a fully or partially fitted bathroom, or whether a simple but well-chosen suite is all that is required. Remember that even the most basic of bathtubs or basins can be embellished with more lavish taps and accessories. You should also take into account the style of decoration in the rest of your home, and decide whether you want your bathroom to be different or have a similar tone.

modern fitted

One of the main practical advantages of a modern fitted bathroom is that there is plenty of storage. This comes in the form of units as well as open shelving, where more attractive items can be displayed to enhance the overall look of the room. This type of bathroom also has a highly decorative finish that lifts the room above the merely functional. Building fixtures such as basins and toilets into a fully fitted design minimizes the visual impact of these utility items, turning them into design features rather than potential eyesores.

RIGHT *You can use the colour scheme of the bathroom units as the basis for the general room decoration to create an attractive, harmonious scheme.*

classical

A classical bathroom design usually has adequate space and simple fittings that are elegant but not necessarily eye-catching. Much of its impact is achieved by choosing fittings that work as a backdrop to other decorative elements in the room – for example, extravagant window dressings, additional furnishings such as chairs and beautiful accessories such as mirrors and flower arrangements. It is the attention to detail on the finishing touches that makes this type of bathroom work.

LEFT *The panelling on the bathtub helps to give this classical, compact bathroom a neat, fitted look. Neutral colours create a comfortable ambience that is enhanced by the natural light enjoyed by the room.*

contemporary unfitted

Achieving a modern look does not mean that you have to adopt a fully fitted or unit-based approach. Instead, you can choose fittings that deviate slightly from traditional styles and arrange them in a more unique and unusual layout. Bathroom manufacturers now produce a huge array of bathroom suites and almost every taste is catered for, so finding something a little quirky should not be too difficult if you opt for this style of bathroom. Again, the general room decoration can help to enhance this look and provide a modern atmosphere (it is a good idea to refer to magazines for the latest colour trends). Decoration also plays an important role in helping to tie the different elements of the room together into a unified whole.

traditional

Traditional bathroom suites generally mirror a certain design period. The suites are often more decorative than their modern counterparts and accessories such as taps can be highly ornamental. Traditional items, such as cabinets, can be combined with this style of suite to enhance the overall look, with an emphasis on furnishings and achieving a comfortable atmosphere.

ABOVE RIGHT *A centrally positioned stud wall creates an unusual but extremely effective bathroom layout.*

RIGHT *The ornamental mirror, rich green tones and decorative window dressing all interact to produce a period-style bathroom with a truly elegant finish.*

BELOW *The innovative designs in every area of this bathroom provide an ultra-modern look that is both functional and of great aesthetic impact.*

designer

'Designer' is a fairly recent term that relates to ultra-modern finishes. These can be truly breathtaking and provide a very individual look. This type of bathroom is usually clean, crisp and minimalist. Such a room can be difficult to maintain in a busy family home, so think carefully about whether it is really suitable before making a final decision. Designer bathroom suites also tend to occupy the more expensive end of the market. However, creating this look successfully can often rely on interesting room features as well as the suite itself, so even if you are on a budget you may be able to achieve this look or something similar.

planning a bathroom

As with all planning and fitting procedures, it is vital that you measure everything accurately if you are to achieve the desired result. This is particularly true of bathrooms, since they often have limited space and you therefore need to know precisely how much room is available when choosing fittings. Be sure to measure every alcove and wall return in order to produce a perfect scale plan. This will enable you to choose the right bathroom suite, both in terms of style and size.

measuring a room

The diagram below is a good example of a scale plan for a bathroom. Although the room is simple in shape, there are a surprising number of areas that have to be measured. As well as the main physical dimensions, you will also need to take into account the positions of electrical points and water supply and drainage pipes, since these will all have an impact on the new design.

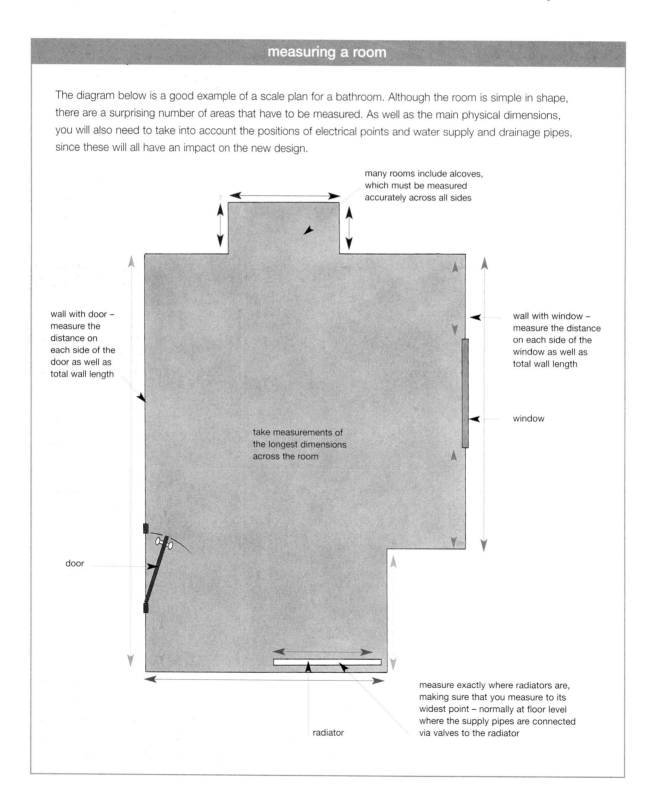

many rooms include alcoves, which must be measured accurately across all sides

wall with door – measure the distance on each side of the door as well as total wall length

wall with window – measure the distance on each side of the window as well as total wall length

window

take measurements of the longest dimensions across the room

door

radiator

measure exactly where radiators are, making sure that you measure to its widest point – normally at floor level where the supply pipes are connected via valves to the radiator

As well as taking the measurements indicated on the diagram opposite, you should also address the following points – bearing in mind that each room will have its own characteristics that you must consider when planning a new bathroom design.

- What is the height of window sills and will this cause a problem when installing fixtures below them?
- Will you be able to open and close the window if a bath or basin is fitted in front of it?
- Is the floor concrete? If so, running cables or supplies underneath is not an option.
- Is the floor constructed from floorboards allowing easy access

for rerouting pipes and cables beneath it?
- Is there easy access above the bathroom so that electric cables can be rerouted easily for any new lighting requirements?
- Are there any steps in the room and is it split-level?
- Are there any stopcocks?
- Is there an extractor fan or will you need to fit one?
- Is the extractor fan in the best position or does it need moving?
- Are there any attractive features, such as arches or small alcoves that can be incorporated into the new bathroom design?
- Does the main door in the room open inwards or outwards?

- Do your measurements on each side of the door take the architrave into account?
- Is the floor sloping, which could make it difficult to install fittings level?
- Has the room previously been used for another purpose? If so, it may have electrical sockets that need removing.
- Is it possible to change old fittings for new without making major alterations to the existing supply and drainage system?
- Can new supplies be boxed in or hidden behind units?
- How easy is it to remove the old fittings from the existing bathroom, and will your new fittings fit through the door frame?

unit & accessory size

Bathroom manufacturers make units and fittings according to a system of standard sizes in order to facilitate the planning and installation. However, when making a scale plan, be sure to use the specific measurements for a particular manufacturer because there may be slight variations. Also, whereas some fittings can be used with a large selection of suites, others are only suited to one design.

👍 tips of the trade

- **Heating –** Make sure there is some provision for radiators or towel rails. It is standard for one or both of these items to be fitted in most bathrooms.

- **Mirrors –** Plan your design so that there is room for a good size mirror, an essential accessory in all bathrooms.

- **Access –** Bathrooms require a great deal of pipework and it is important that pipes can be accessed in case of emergency. Any boxing or panelling should be built so that pipework can be inspected if necessary.

making a plan

The importance of taking accurate measurements cannot be over-stressed, and it is essential that you draw a precise scale diagram to ensure that any new furnishings and fixtures you are planning to buy will fit into the room. The plan must take into account all the questions and considerations discussed above and opposite, as well as the points covered on pages 12–13 regarding the general shape of the room.

Once you have taken all the measurements, use graph paper to draw an accurate overhead plan of

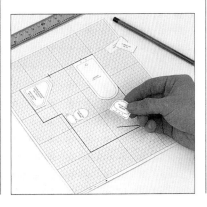

the room. This will be of immense value when designing the new layout of the area. Some manufacturers even provide ready-made scale cut-outs of their products so that you can work out the best possible layout.

If you take your measurements along to a manufacturer, they usually offer a planning service that provides a detailed plan of the bathroom, including side as well as overhead elevations. This will give you a better idea of how the finished bathroom will look. They can also give advice on the planning procedure when installing a new bathroom suite, so it is always a good idea to make use of this service, even if you do not buy as many items as the manufacturer may offer.

Also bear in mind that bathroom showrooms always feature a number of displays of different styles of suite. This can help you get a feel for what a particular suite may look like in your own bathroom and is an invaluable aid to achieving the right look.

choosing styles

Choosing bathroom fittings is in many ways similar to choosing other household furnishings in the sense that a bathroom suite plays no structural role in your home   your choice of suite can, therefore, be based purely on style preferences. There are numerous options available, and it is important to be aware of the way that different styles of fitting may fulfil your particular needs. A number of simple designs common to most bathrooms are shown here.

units

Units provide storage and can be used to house bathroom suite items to create a fully fitted look. Doors and drawer fronts can be selected from a wide range of designs and fixed to the unit carcasses.

heated towel rails

Modern towel rails are usually designed to be unobtrusive. Chrome is a popular choice of finish, although more vibrant colours are available. Traditional rails are suitable in a classical bathroom design. A small radiator may be combined with the pipework that makes up the rail.

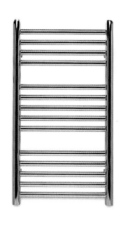

baths

roll-top

Roll-top baths are the traditional choice. Although they can be expensive, their renewed popularity has led to more competitive prices.

standard

Standard baths offer the best value for money because they are mass produced. They still take up the largest sector of the market.

corner

Corner baths provide an attractive alternative that has a hint of luxury. Smaller varieties are also ideal in bathrooms where space is limited.

toilets

high-level & low-level

High-level toilets, so called because the cistern is positioned high above the toilet and connected to it by a long supply pipe, follow an old-fashioned design that has become popular once more for those bathrooms that have a traditional look. Low-level toilets have the cistern positioned above the toilet pan but with a far shorter supply pipe than in the high-level example shown here. Bear in mind the extra wall space requirements if you choose this type of traditional design.

close-couple

This is the most modern toilet design, with the cistern positioned directly on top of the toilet pan with no separate supply pipe between the two items. This design takes up much less room and is also far easier to install than the high- or low-level options. Some manufacturers even produce cisterns that can be fitted into a corner so that the toilet can be situated pointing directly out from the corner of the room, which adds an interesting feature as well as saving space.

bidets

There are two main bidet designs: over-rim supply and rim supply. Over-rim supply bidets have less stringent regulations regarding fitting procedures.

basins

pedestal

Pedestal basins are popular because the pedestal section can be used both to hide pipework and to support the weight of the basin.

wall-mounted

Wall-mounted basins rely on strong fixings to support their weight. Hiding pipework can be tricky but the final look is well worth the work involved.

corner

Manufacturers also produce corner basins. These save space and, as such, represent a suitable choice for smaller bathrooms.

choosing fittings

Having chosen the larger bathroom fixtures that comprise the main part of the suite, you can then select the smaller fittings and accessories such as taps, shelving and towel rings. Many bathroom suite manufacturers will recommend particular fittings for particular suites, but it is always possible to choose other options as long as you check compatibility. This is particularly important with taps, which can vary considerably.

taps

Tap function, quality and price are all important when making a selection because there is such an enormous range available that it can sometimes be difficult to make a final decision. The starting point is always to narrow down the choice to those fittings that are compatible with your suite. It is at this stage that final comparisons can be drawn and issues of preference and suitability taken into account.

Tap finishes vary from chrome- and gold-plate effects to solid plate taps – the overall quality is usually reflected in the price. Also remember that you need to choose waste outlets, and the main question here is whether you select a pop-up waste or a more traditional chain and plug. The style of finish of the outlet usually complements the tap design. Below are a few examples of tap designs and waste outlets.

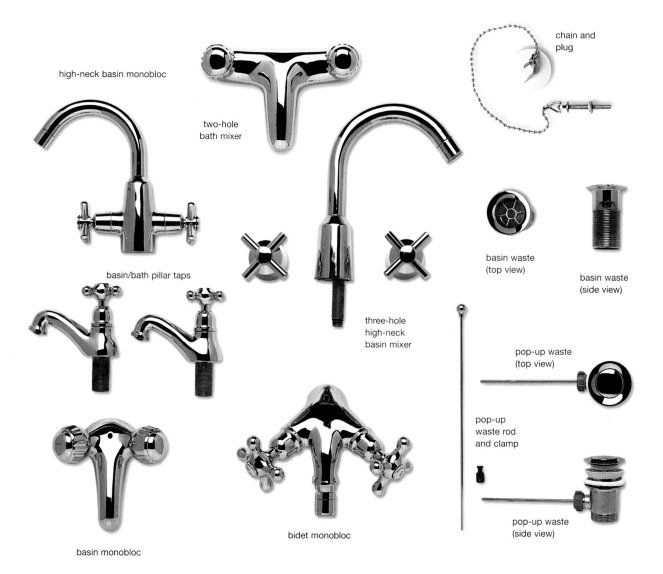

high-neck basin monobloc

two-hole bath mixer

chain and plug

basin/bath pillar taps

three-hole high-neck basin mixer

basin waste (top view)

basin waste (side view)

pop-up waste (top view)

pop-up waste rod and clamp

pop-up waste (side view)

basin monobloc

bidet monobloc

Holders and accessories are available in sets so that you can achieve a well-planned, harmonious look. Although these accessories are usually the last items to be fitted during a renovation, it is important to make choices at an early stage so that you can build up a picture in your own mind of what the finished bathroom will look like, and how different fittings and features will be coordinated. Although all these items have a functional role to play, their aesthetics are just as important to the decorative impact of the room. In many cases minimalist designs are the most suitable choice, but more ornate examples can provide a 'lift' to a bathroom should more decorative adornment be desired. Also to the right are two examples of non-heated towel rails (heated rails are shown on pages 26–27), which are generally situated above radiators.

OTHER ACCESSORIES

• **Cabinets –** Many bathroom designs incorporate a cabinet for storing toiletries. This cabinet may also be used to hold medicines, in which case it must be out of the reach of children and/or locked for safety reasons. Choices of cabinets are shown in greater detail on pages 74–75.

• **Movable items –** When looking for bathroom accessories, you need to give some thought to whether movable items will play any part in your design. In much the same way that accessories such as tumbler and toothbrush holders can be bought as sets, there are other movable items such as toilet brushes, bathroom scales and freestanding mirrors that can be chosen to complement other features in the room.

chrome bracket supports with glass tumbler and soap dish

ceramic tumbler and toothbrush holder with glass tumbler

chrome towel ring

chrome toilet roll holder

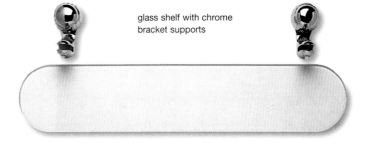

glass shelf with chrome bracket supports

chrome towel rail with chrome support brackets

chrome towel rail with ceramic support brackets

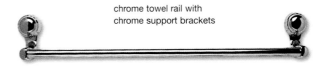

soap dish tile

ceramic soap dish

choosing fittings

29

choosing showers

Showers have become an essential part of most modern bathrooms, whether installed as a separate unit or positioned above a bath. The pace of modern living means that a shower is often chosen in preference to a taking bath. It is also more environmentally friendly because less water is used to achieve the same results. All these advantages have meant that showers have increased in popularity, which in turn has led to greater manufacturing innovation and choice.

types of shower

When deciding upon the type of shower to fit, your first consideration should be whether it is suitable for your home plumbing system. For example, many showers are gravity fed – in other words, the water tank needs to be situated at least 1m (1yd) above the shower in order to provide the required water pressure. An extra pump can be installed to create a 'power' shower if desired. Electric showers are another option and have a separate electrical unit to heat up mains-supply water on demand. In addition, manufacturers are always developing new designs. It is, therefore, always advisable to take professional advice when choosing a shower so that you get the best system for your needs.

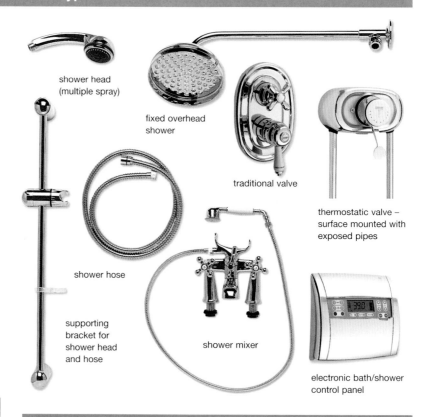

shower head (multiple spray)

fixed overhead shower

traditional valve

thermostatic valve – surface mounted with exposed pipes

shower hose

supporting bracket for shower head and hose

shower mixer

electronic bath/shower control panel

SPRAY FUNCTIONS

One important consideration when choosing a shower is whether the head has a number of spray functions. These provide a choice in the way the water is expelled from the head in terms of direction and strength of flow.

multiple spray shower head

single spray shower head

showers in baths

Positioning a shower above a bath is the most popular type of a shower facility because it saves a great deal of space and does not require any additional plumbing to get rid of waste water. You will need to install a good quality screen or shower curtain to prevent overspray onto the bathroom floor. A power shower produces more overspray and so a longer screen may be required.

RIGHT *A folding shower screen allows normal access to the bath when the shower is not in use.*

For separate showers, the shower system itself is generally housed inside some sort of cubicle. These vary considerably in design, as do the actual shower trays. In most cases, a particular shape of tray fits a specific shape of cubicle, but you will still need to decide upon the depth of tray. For example, a shallow tray can appear more aesthetically pleasing than deeper options but it will mean that drainage outlets and waste pipes will need to be below floor level, in which case you must consider whether this is either suitable or possible for your bathroom. Another thing to consider if you opt for a power shower is that the cubicle and tray design must be able to deal with the high-pressure force of the water. Power showers expel more water more quickly than conventional showers, so the tray can fill up unless the drainage outlet has sufficient capacity to take away the waste water. In addition, the cubicle must be sealed so that the upwards force of water from shower jets hitting the tray does not cause any leaks.

corner entry – hinged door on pentagonal tray

corner entry – sliding door

side entry – pivotal door

side entry – bi-folding door

quadrant-shaped tray and cubicle

three-sided cubicle with pivoting door

streamline resin stone tray

acrylic raised tray

resin stone corner tray (pentagon)

shower curtains & screens

When a shower unit is positioned above a bath some type of barrier is required to prevent overspray from the shower hitting the bathroom floor. Fitting a shower curtain is one of the most popular options, especially since a curtain can be tied back out of the way when not in use and is relatively inexpensive to replace. Shower screens represent the more sturdy option, are easier to keep clean and will need replacing much less frequently than a shower curtain. There are many different shapes, designs and fixing mechanisms – the main choice will be whether you want a fixed screen or a folding screen.

clear hinged screen

patterned hinged screen

order of work

Carrying out any home improvement project requires a sensible order of work so that tasks can be completed to the correct standard and as quickly and efficiently as possible. Since bathrooms are in everyday use, it is important to plan events carefully so that the least possible disruption is caused to daily life. You need to consider a number of factors if you are to ensure a smooth and efficient renovation procedure.

budgeting

Buying new bathroom fittings and accessories is generally a straightforward purchase that is easy to budget for because the manufacturer will provide a fixed price. However, on top of this basic cost you will need to account for all the extras detailed below, which can substantially inflate the budget:

- hiring professional tradespeople e.g. for connecting and disconnecting plumbing and electrics or for major construction work
- general redecoration of the room – the major expense here is usually tiling walls
- laying new flooring material or renovating existing floorboards
- any structural work to be undertaken for larger renovation jobs e.g. creating an en-suite bathroom by either building a new stud partition or knocking through a wall to join two separate rooms
- commissioning architectural drawings and employing a surveyor if carrying out substantial construction work that involves major structural change
- any unforeseen changes or problems encountered once the work has begun – add a further 10–15% on top of your final figure

schedule of work

From start to finish, bathroom installation can take longer than you may first have thought. However, as long as water supplies are not cut for any long period of time, and essential appliances are changed over in the same day, the bathroom can still be used for necessary tasks so that the household will continue to function during this period of upheaval. For planning purposes it is important to have an accurate idea of the timescale for the entire bathroom renovation project. The following factors must be taken into account when drawing up a schedule of work:

- on large projects where a whole bathroom is to be fitted, it is unlikely that the time between order and delivery will be less than four weeks
- most manufacturers will be able to give a rough guide for the time it will take to install the bathroom suite, but it is always worth adding several extra days on top to account for any problems
- once delivered most new bathrooms can be fitted in a week, but the time taken will clearly depend on size and the degree of complication in the layout
- plan for two to three days preparation prior to delivery (more if building work is required)
- plan for a week after the installation for laying the floor and general decoration
- tradespeople will need to be organized into a workable time frame – plumbers or electricians will probably need to visit twice, once to adjust connections on the old bathroom and once to reconnect the new – coordinate the timing of your work so that they may be booked in advance for the slots you require
- waste disposal is a job that is often overlooked but must also be accounted for in the schedule of work e.g. a skip will probably need to be hired to take all the bits and pieces that comprised the old bathroom away and you will need to dispose of the packaging used for the new bathroom

dealing with professionals

Decisions will need to be made concerning the extent of the work that you intend and are able to carry out yourself, and the areas where professional help may be required. At some stage it is likely that you will need to contact plumbers or electricians for specific jobs. Bear in mind the following guidelines when hiring professionals and negotiating a price for the work:

- when choosing a professional, always get a personal recommendation – scanning classified advertisements for a random tradesperson is a sure recipe for disaster and should always be avoided
- always get a 'price' – tradespeople who produce 'estimates' or 'quotations' should be viewed with some caution as the vagueness of the term allows scope for boosting the bill at the end of the job, whereas an initial 'price' provides good grounds for understanding that this will be the final figure you pay
- the cost for work to be carried out should not change unless you alter specifications for the work
- never offer to pay tradespeople up front, as this can encourage them to neglect the project – if money is to be paid once work is completed this is a greater incentive for them to stay on site
- for larger jobs it is reasonable to pay in stages, just make sure each installment is dependent upon completion of an agreed amount of work
- if expensive materials need to be bought it is acceptable for the tradesperson to expect that these costs will be met prior to installation
- tradespeople will usually need to be hired for disconnecting the old bathroom and reconnecting the new – when they offer a quote for the job, make it clear that two visits will be required
- once you have hired a tradesperson, try to get as much advice from them as possible regarding any preparatory work so that their jobs are straightforward when they arrive for work

dealing with manufacturers

Manufacturers will usually only be involved in a bathroom renovation project prior to actual installation, when you are working out the design and choosing styles, although some can also be hired for installation. When dealing with a manufacturer to finalize the design of your bathroom, negotiate a price and organize delivery, you will need to consider the following issues:

- as discussed on pages 24–5, it is essential to measure accurately so that a detailed plan may be provided for both you and a manufacturer to decide on the best layout and finish for a new bathroom suite
- ascertain from the start whether your chosen accessories and appliances can be fitted into your design
- sales representatives are generally well trained and will provide good service, but remember to check for any hidden extras in a bathroom specification and ensure that you are being quoted for all the components that make up the bathroom you desire, e.g. check that plinth, cornice and end panels are included in the price and make sure that handles for doors and drawers are not extra
- most manufacturers will also offer deals, providing free items according to the amount of money you spend – this can obviously be to your advantage, but check that the initial unit price has not been artificially inflated to account for these 'give aways' and ensure that such items are the correct specification for your needs
- if you are employing the manufacturer to fit the entire bathroom they will provide a price for the work at the time the suite is ordered – this is normally quite competitive since it forms part of an overall package, but it can still be worth approaching an independent trader to see what price they are prepared to offer
- once a deal has been done, confirm a delivery date – it is rarely possible to buy a bathroom 'off the shelf' and there is normally a time delay between the purchase and actual delivery of units and accessories
- when the units and accessories are delivered you will be surprised by the amount of pieces that are supplied for a fitted bathroom suite – check and double-check the delivery to ensure that everything has arrived and, most importantly, that no items are damaged, so that you can immediately report back to the manufacturer

tools & materials

A basic tool kit is essential for home improvement work, it needs to contain general construction and multi-purpose tools appropriate for a number of tasks around the home. For dealing with bathrooms, this tool kit will need to include items more specifically directed towards bathroom renovation, for example, you will need to have the correct tools for undertaking some minor plumbing work. You may also need to purchase some particular construction materials.

general tools

It is always best to opt for quality when building up a general tool kit, as these tend to be the items that you will use most for home improvements. Although spending a little extra on quality tools is no absolute guarantee that they will last, it is a better option than settling for the cheapest tools that almost certainly will not stand up to the tests of time.

claw hammer

bradawl

nail punch

pipe, joist and cable detector

slot-head screwdrivers

cross head screwdrivers

insulated sleeves

club hammer

bolster chisel

combination pliers

side cutters

long-nose pliers

half-round rasp

general purpose chisels

mini level

cordless drill/driver

carpenter's pencil

tape measure

sealant dispenser

stepladder

clamp

combination square

hacksaw

mitresaw

pointing trowel

panel saw

plastic bucket

craft knife

workbench

power tools

The market for power tools is continually expanding and prices have fallen dramatically in recent years. It is, therefore, worth considering building up a good power tool kit, especially if you plan to do more than the odd bit of DIY. These are some of the more useful power tools to have, although you can now buy items for tackling any number of specific cutting or fixing jobs around the home.

power drill

jigsaw

router

electric sander

HIRING TOOLS
For isolated tasks that may require particularly heavy-duty equipment, or tools that are very expensive to buy, hiring is often the best option. This area has become a growing sector of the DIY market, and hire shops are increasingly catering for home repair enthusiasts.

plumbing tools

It is best to buy just the basic items that will be required for the general plumbing jobs you may come across during a bathroom renovation. Only tackle plumbing tasks if you are certain of the correct procedures and seek professional advice if you have any reservations.

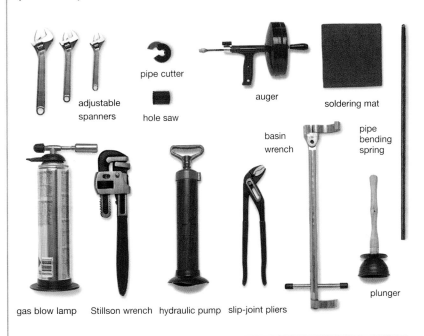

pipe cutter

adjustable spanners

hole saw

auger

soldering mat

basin wrench

pipe bending spring

gas blow lamp   Stillson wrench   hydraulic pump   slip-joint pliers

plunger

materials

Materials should always be purchased according to their requirement for particular jobs, but some items are always useful to have handy as they are frequently used in bathroom renovation or repair projects. This basic materials kit may then be supplemented according to the specific job being tackled.

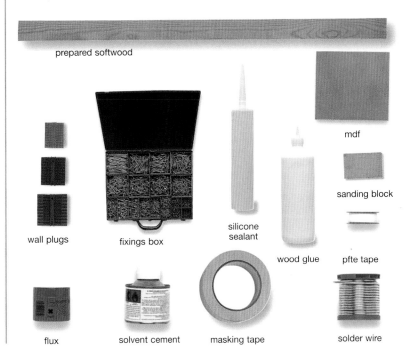

prepared softwood

mdf

wall plugs   fixings box

silicone sealant

sanding block

wood glue   pfte tape

flux   solvent cement   masking tape   solder wire

fitting bathrooms

Installing a new bathroom, with all the relevant fixtures and fittings, requires a certain amount of skill. There will probably be some areas where you need to seek professional advice, but as far as the basic tasks are concerned, most jobs are relatively straightforward as long as the correct order of work is followed and appropriate techniques used. This chapter outlines the various types of pipes and fittings that you are likely to encounter and shows the best techniques for installing a wide selection of fittings. Be sure to plan jobs thoroughly so that you have all the right connections for a particular installation before you start.

Bathroom fixtures, such as the toilet and bath shown here, need to be assembled, then positioned and plumbed in.

preparing the bathroom ⁄⁄⁄⁄

The amount of preparation required will depend on whether you are fitting an entirely new bathroom suite or simply replacing one or two items. In nearly all cases you will need to switch off water supplies while the changeover takes place. Where the position of fittings is to be changed radically from the existing layout, you will also need to reroute pipes (see also pages 40–3). However, the first thing to do is turn off the water and remove the old fittings.

tools for the job

screwdriver

basin wrench

adjustable spanners

shutting off water

Before embarking on any bathroom renovation project, it is essential that you have a sound understanding of how water supplies can be turned off. All houses have a series of stopcocks and valves that allow water supplies to be turned off quickly in an emergency or for the simple purpose of changing fittings. Older houses tend to have fewer stopcocks than newer homes, where you will find that most fittings have shut-off valves located in close proximity to them so that they can be isolated from the rest of the water supply.

Stopcocks – also called gate valves or shut-off valves – are nothing more than taps used to close or open water supplies. They are located at different positions along water supply pipes, with the main stopcock generally located close to where the water comes into the house – it is often positioned in the kitchen below the sink. Turning this off will shut down the cold water supply. In most cases there is also a storage tank for the hot water supply. You will need to find the appropriate stopcock to shut off the water supply to and/or from the tank in order to avoid having to drain the entire hot water system.

Shut-off valves are always positioned close to fittings but the way in which they are turned on and off can vary. In some cases, as shown here, a slot-head screwdriver is used to open and close the valve. Some valve designs have a small handle, which eliminates the need for a screwdriver.

safety advice

If in any doubt about how to use stopcocks to control water supply, always seek professional advice.

disconnecting basins

1 Shut down the water supply to the basin, then turn on the hot and cold taps to allow any water left in them to drain away. Use a basin wrench to undo the nuts connecting the supply pipes to the tap tails.

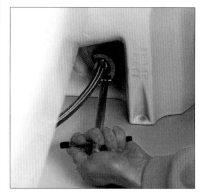

2 If you are replacing the whole basin, there is no need to disconnect the taps any further and you can proceed straight to step 3. If you are only replacing the taps use the basin wrench to undo the tap backnuts. This will release the taps from their position in the basin.

3 Disconnect the waste pipe from the basin by unscrewing the trap. Designs vary from basin to basin, but because the drainage pipe and trap are generally connected with several threaded joints, it is always possible to find a joint that is easy to unscrew.

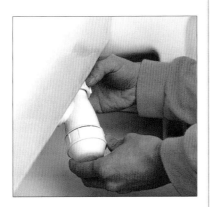

4 Undo the retaining screws that hold the basin against the wall – these are usually found on the underside of the sink. If there is a pedestal, this should support the weight of the sink while you carry out this procedure. A wall-mounted basin may have a bracket support, but if it does not, ask a helper to take the weight of the basin while you undo the fixing screws.

disconnecting toilets

The technique for disconnecting a toilet will vary slightly according to design but, once again, the most important thing is to shut off the water supply to the cistern before

beginning work. In this example, a close-coupled toilet and cistern is being removed.

1 Turn off the water supply, then flush the toilet to remove any water from the cistern before disconnecting the supply pipe.

2 Undo the retaining nuts on the underside of the cistern that hold it in place on the toilet pan.

3 Where necessary, remove the retaining screws inserted through the back of the cistern that hold it in place on the wall.

4 Lift the cistern free of the toilet pan and put it to one side. Take care when lifting it as it may be quite heavy.

5 Undo the retaining screws or bolts at the base of the pan. The toilet may now be eased out of place, ready for the new one to be installed. Temporarily block the soil pipe opening with a cloth to keep sewer gases at bay.

DISCONNECTING BATHS

Baths are disconnected in a similar way to basins. Begin by closing the shut-off valves, then disconnect the supply and waste pipes. Bathtubs with feet may need unscrewing from the floor and, in many cases, the framework for a bath panel may have to be removed so that the bath can be eased free. Baths can be very heavy, especially the older, cast-iron varieties, so two people will be required to lift the bath free after it has been disconnected.

preparing plumbing & electrics ⁄⁄⁄⁄

When new fittings are to be positioned in a different place from the old ones, you will need to reroute supplies. It is therefore important to have some understanding of the different types of pipe available and the various ways in which they can be joined. Before embarking on any pipework, always turn off the water supply and drain the pipes. In terms of electrical supplies, major overhauls are not usually required in a bathroom, although some cables may need rerouting.

cutting copper pipes

tools for the job

pipe cutter

wire wool

1 Clamp the pipe cutter around the pipe and rotate it in the direction designated by the arrow until it cuts all the way through. You can use a hacksaw to cut the pipe if you wish, but a pipe cutter gives a cleaner cut.

2 Clean the pipe using wire wool before making any connection.

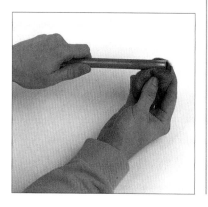

connecting copper pipes

There are several ways of making a connection or joint between copper pipes. The simplest is to insert a compression joint. However, it may be unsightly if it is in a position that can be easily viewed. The other methods involve using solder and a gas torch. They are slightly more difficult but produce a neater finish.

compression joints

Compression joints are easy to fit because the process does not require the use of a gas torch.

tools for the job

adjustable spanners

1 Separate the compression fitting and slip it in place on the two ends of the cut pipe. To begin with, position it hand tight with the olives (small rings) situated on the pipe inside the fitting.

tips of the trade

Pipe connectors are made in many different shapes, for example elbow joints and T-connectors, so that it is possible to reroute most pipes.

2 Use adjustable spanners to tighten the joint, allowing the threaded section to tighten onto the olives to create a watertight seal.

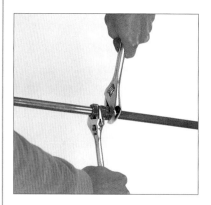

solder ring joints

Solder ring joints are the easiest type of joint to make because the solder itself is already inside the connector.

tools for the job

gas torch

heat-resistant mat

1 Apply flux to the ends of the pipes and inside the connector. The flux helps to clean the copper and achieve a watertight joint.

2 Slot both ends of the pipe into the connector. Holding the pipe over a heat-resistant mat, use a gas torch to heat the joint gently, allowing the solder ring inside it to melt and form a watertight seal.

safety advice

When using a gas torch, always read the manufacturer's guidelines to ensure safe use. Gas torches should never be left burning unattended and a heat-resistant mat should be positioned next to the joint to avoid burning or singeing adjacent surfaces.

end feed joints

The other type of solder joint is referred to as an end feed joint. It does not contain a ring of solder inside and, therefore, the solder must be applied during the heating procedure with the gas torch. Flux is still used to clean pipe ends, but solder wire must be applied around the joint to create a watertight seal.

connecting plastic pipes

Plastic pipes are usually very easy to connect since many have push-fit joints or are threaded with rubber washers. However, in some cases solvent weld joints have to be formed using a special type of cement to fix the pipes together.

tools for the job

hacksaw or hand saw

cloth

1 Cut the pipes to the required size with a hacksaw or hand saw and clean the ends thoroughly.

2 Apply solvent weld cement around the end of the pipe. Push the end of the pipe into the required connector. Remove excess cement with a cloth and allow the joint to dry before continuing with the next section.

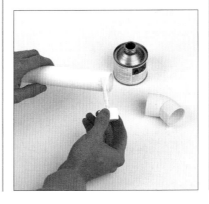

electrical rerouting

In hollow walls or ceiling voids, cables can be fed into place, but with solid walls the procedure is more laborious. Leave the actual electrical work, such as wiring, to professionals.

tools for the job

club hammer

bolster chisel

hammer

protective equipment

1 Draw pencil guidelines where the cable will run. Use a club hammer and bolster chisel to cut through the wall, removing material to a depth of around 2.5cm (1in).

2 Position the cable well below surface level. Cover it with an impact-resistant plastic channel held in place with galvanized nails, then apply a surface finish such as plaster.

plastic plumbing

Although copper pipe is still used as the main type of water supply pipe in the home, plastic pipe is becoming much more commonplace because the way they are jointed makes them incredibly easy to work with. Pipe and fitting designs can vary slightly between manufacturers, so it is best to use the same type of plastic plumbing throughout your home. However, all manufacturers produce adaptors to join their plastic pipes with the more conventional copper pipe systems.

tools for the job

pipe cutter or mini hacksaw
adjustable spanners
screwdriver
cordless drill/driver

cutting & joining plastic

Before you can build up any sort of plastic supply pipe system, you need to understand how to form a simple joint or connection between two lengths of pipe.

1 Plastic supply pipe can be cut with any fine-toothed saw – a mini hacksaw is ideal. Alternatively, you can buy proprietary cutters. Whatever you use, try to make the cut as square as possible. Remove rough edges with fine abrasive paper.

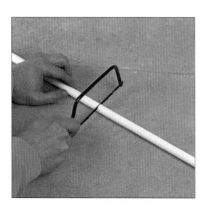

2 Push both ends of the pipe into the ends of the connector. Push each pipe in as far as it will go, making sure they have both been grabbed by the rings inside the joint.

3 Pull the pipes away from the joint to create a watertight seal.

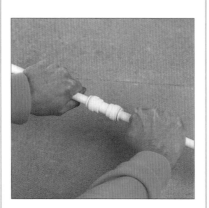

4 If you need to undo the joint for any reason, simply push the end collar on the joint to loosen it and pull the pipe free from the fitting.

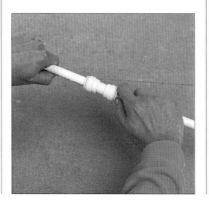

joining copper & plastic

Joining a section of copper and plastic pipe together can be achieved very simply using a specially designed adaptor. It is fitted in a similar way to a compression joint.

1 Fit one section of a copper compression joint onto the end of the copper pipe and remove the securing nut from the other end of the joint.

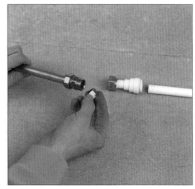

2 Fit the plastic adaptor onto the copper compression joint and use adjustable spanners to tighten the joint and make it watertight.

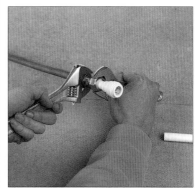

3 Insert and secure the plastic pipe as shown in steps 2 and 3 of 'cutting & joining plastic' on the opposite page.

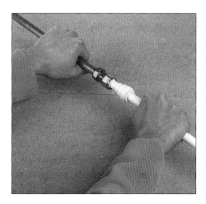

fitting a shut-off valve

Shut-off valves are available for both copper and plastic pipes. Designs vary ÷ the one shown here is operated by a slot-head screwdriver.

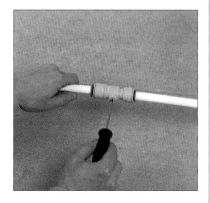

inserting a stop end

It is sometimes necessary to close off the end of a pipe. For example, when changing bathroom fittings there may be a time delay between removing the old fitting and installing the new one. Therefore the water may have to be turned back on in the meantime to provide a supply for other areas in the house. Whatever the reason, the method used is to push a stop end into the opening of the pipe and then pull it back to secure it in place.

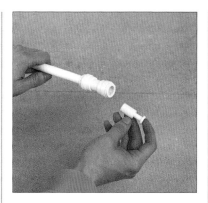

using reducers

When a larger bore of pipe needs to be joined to a smaller bore, use reducers to connect them. Reducers are manufactured in all sizes to cope with a variety of needs.

1 Insert the end of the reducer into a connector for the larger pipe bore. Pull it back to lock it in position.

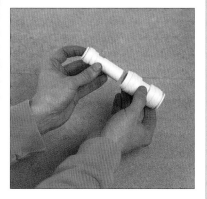

2 Insert the small bore pipe into the reducer and pull it back to lock it in position. Insert the larger bore pipe into the large bore.

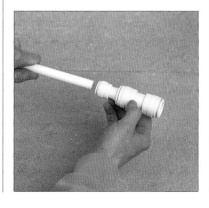

supporting pipes

All supply pipes have to be supported at intervals along the course of their route. However, because plastic pipe is more flexible than copper pipe, more clips are needed to provide adequate support to the pipe once the water supply is in use.

1 Position pipe clips along the route of the pipe at intervals of no more than 30cm (1ft).

2 Make sure that the pipe is clipped firmly in place before the water is turned on so that there is no danger of the pipes sagging and thereby placing joints under unnecessary stress.

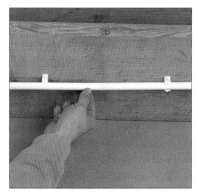

tips of the trade

To ensure that clips are aligned, use a spirit level to draw a pencil line along the joists to act as a fixing guideline.

installing fitted bathroom units ⚒

Fitted bathroom units are becoming increasingly common. They are sometimes supplied ready-assembled but, in many cases, they are flat-packed and require assembly before being installed. Some units are designed to form part of a run of units, while others, such as a vanity unit, are used singly as separate features. Whatever the case, the principles for assembly are similar. Many flat-packs are put together using cam studs and plastic connecting blocks, as shown here.

tools for the job

hammer

screwdriver

cordless drill/driver

1 Organization is the key to assembling units – so lay out all the relevant sections to make sure you have the required number of components and the correct fixings to put them together. Follow the manufacturer's guidelines for assembly – in most cases, the first step is to hammer plastic connectors into pre-drilled holes along the edges of the panels. In this case, the connectors are being inserted in the two side panels of the unit.

2 Insert wooden dowels into the appropriate holes on the edges of the shelving sections. Insert cam screws into the pre-drilled holes, pushing them in position by hand and making sure the open end of the screw thread is pointing towards the edge of the shelf or unit section. Insert the cam studs that will attach

to the screws in the corresponding part of the unit. Some may need a turn of the screwdriver to fit them securely in place. Since the pre-drilled holes have been accurately made in a factory, cam studs and screws offer an efficient connection mechanism that ensures precision and eliminates the chance of errors.

3 Assemble the unit by marrying the corresponding sections at the appropriate fixing points. The cam studs connect with the cam screws by inserting the stud into the screw, then turning the screw to lock the fixing in place. Continue to add sections of the unit until the basic carcass is complete.

4 Now work on the unit doors. Most manufacturers use recessed hinges that are hidden from external view when the door is closed. Their exact positions are generally pre-marked and cut into the back of the doors, so fitting is a simple process of positioning the hinge and screwing it in place.

5 Hinge plates may also be attached to the carcass of the unit, again using the pre-drilled holes made in the manufacturing process. Most hinge plates are reversible but in some cases there is a right and wrong way up, so always check before attaching them to make sure that the door hinges will fit.

6 Fit the doors in place by hooking the hinges onto the hinge plates and tightening the central retaining screw to hold them in position. These types of hinges are always adjustable, so once the unit is in place it is still possible to move the door position slightly to make sure they are level and open and close correctly, although it usually takes a little trial and error to get them right.

7 Now fit the basin section of the unit. In this case, the moulded basin section is screwed in place using the plastic connecting blocks on the edge of the carcass. Screws are inserted through the blocks into a chipboard section that is an integral part of the basin unit. There will inevitably be variations between manufacturers regarding how the basin is fitted, so it is important to follow their guidelines.

8 With this unit a drawer front is used to finish the front section, which that is held in place with connecting blocks.

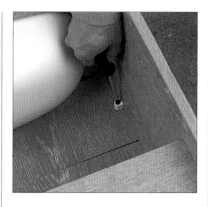

9 You will need to make some sort of provision at the back edge of the carcass for fixing the unit to the wall. L-shaped brackets are ideal for this purpose and are usually supplied by the manufacturer as part of the flat-pack. Screw them into position along the back edge of the unit.

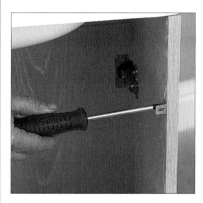

10 Attach door handles by drilling through the door at the marked points. Be sure to use an appropriate size drill bit or the handles will be loose. To prevent splitting or damaging the doors, hold a block of wood at the position where the drill bit will re-emerge from the door.

11 Screw the handles in place using one hand to hold the handle while the other hand operates the screwdriver.

LEVELLING A RUN OF UNITS

In many cases it will be necessary to connect a number of units in a row. In such circumstances, assemble the units separately and position them along the wall, using a spirit level to check that they are correctly aligned horizontally and/or vertically, according to the planned layout of the room. A 2m (2yd) spirit level is particularly useful for this job because it can span several units, making this procedure much easier.

FINISHING TOUCHES

Once the unit is assembled, it can be positioned against the wall. If necessary – for example, for a vanity unit, as shown here – make sure that the relevant water supply and drainage outlets are ready for connection. You will also need to install the fittings for the basin (this is covered in greater detail later in the chapter). It is often best to fit taps to a unit before it is installed in its final position so that you can gain easy access to the underside of the basin. When you have completed all of the above, final fitting is a case of doing up connections and securing the unit in position against the wall.

installing a basin & pedestal

Most of the hard work involved in installing a basin and pedestal is concerned with making sure that the water supply pipes and waste pipe are appropriately located for easy connection. If you are merely replacing a basin, you will usually be able to reuse the existing supplies and waste when it comes to reconnection. However, if the new basin is situated in a different area to the original basin position, it will be necessary to adjust the lengths of the supply and waste pipes, as discussed earlier in this chapter (see pages 40–1 and 44–5).

monobloc taps & pop-up wastes

Whatever the type of taps or waste being fitted, the basic technique for installing a basin and pedestal remains the same. It is best to attach the taps and waste to the basin before fixing the basin to the wall, as it is much easier to gain access. In this case, a monobloc tap and pop-up waste are being fitted.

tools for the job

slip-joint pliers

screwdriver

spirit level

1 Position the sealing washer at the base of the tap, so that a watertight seal will be formed when the tap is positioned on the basin. If the taps you are using are not supplied with a washer, apply silicone sealant around the base of the tap before fitting it in place.

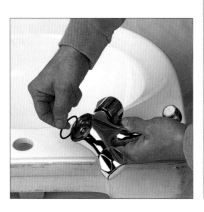

2 Fit the copper supply pipes by screwing them into the base of the tap. A rubber washer is generally supplied to form a tight seal between the threaded part of the supply pipe and the tap. You will also need to insert the threaded bolt, which is used to hold the tap in position.

3 Thread the supply pipes and threaded bolt through the hole in the basin. Position a rubber gasket on the underside of the basin hole, followed by a retainer ring, threading both over the threaded bolt. Secure them with a lock nut, which can be done by hand but may need tightening with pliers. Do not over-tighten.

tips of the trade

Basins can easily be chipped or cracked, especially when working on a concrete floor, so you should always protect the basin by laying a dust sheet on the floor.

4 Attention may now be turned to the waste. A pop-up waste system is constructed from a number of components. Thread the top section of the waste outlet through the outlet in the basin ensuring that the correct gasket has been fitted over the outlet tail. If a gasket is not supplied with the outlet, the waste may be seated on silicone sealant. If using sealant, be sure to wipe away any excess before it dries.

5 Screw the bottom section of the waste in place on the underside of the outlet. Once again, ensure the correct gasket has been positioned between the waste section and the underside of the basin outlet. Do not over-tighten, just make sure the waste is securely fitted and watertight.

6 Insert the pop-up waste rod and screw the waste lever into the base of the waste outlet. Fix the waste lever with a threaded nut, which is secured hand tight.

7 Join the lever and pop-up waste rod with the supplied clamp by threading the rod and lever into two retaining holes in the clamp. Fix the rod and lever firmly in place with two well-tightened screws.

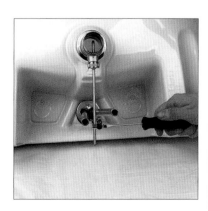

8 Position the basin pedestal in front of and covering any supply pipes. Until the basin is in place and levelled up you will not be able to

position the pedestal exactly. However, positioning the pedestal before the basin will ensure a good contact between the two, making the overall placement as secure as possible.

9 Carefully lift and position the basin on top of the pedestal, adjusting pedestal position to ensure the basin sits correctly. Use a spirit level to check the basin is level, with its back face flush against the wall.

10 Fix the basin in place with retaining screws inserted through the back of the basin and into the wall surface. If it is a solid wall,

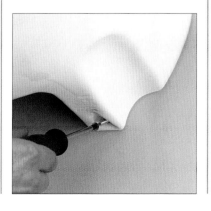

you may need to use wall plugs. Over-tightened screws may crack the basin, so use a hand-held screwdriver for greater control.

11 Secure the pedestal through the holes inside the base. Do not over-tighten and make sure the screws are long enough to hold firm in the floor, but not so long that they damage underfloor services.

12 Position the waste bung adjusting the level so it will provide a watertight seal. Connect up the outlet and water supply pipes, before turning on the water supply.

ALTERNATIVE TAP DESIGNS

Some taps have tails that connect to the water supply with braided steel supply tubes. These tails are secured in place with backnuts on the basin, before the supply tube is attached. You will still require a gasket and/or washer barrier between the metal surfaces of the tap and the basin.

installing a wall-mounted basin ////

There is little difference between a wall-mounted basin and a basin and pedestal in terms of connections and function. The different installation processes centre around the way in which the basin is fixed to the wall, and the manner in which supply and drainage pipes are either hidden or made more decorative. This need to hide supplies can make installing a wall-mounted basin awkward because access to connections is more limited.

solid walls

You need to provide an appropriate route for the required pipes to reach the basin. In a solid wall, this involves chasing out a channel.

tools for the job

tape measure
pencil
spirit level
club hammer
bolster chisel
protective equipment

1 Mark the basin position on the wall and draw pencil guidelines down the wall to demarcate a channel to accommodate pipes. Allow space for connecting with existing supplies.

2 Use a club hammer and bolster chisel to remove this channel. Wear gloves and goggles to protect from flying debris. Once the channel is deep enough, supply pipes may be routed to the correct position.

hollow walls

Pipework can be routed through the cavity in hollow walls. However, access holes often need to be so large to accomplish this that cutting out a section of plasterboard may be the easiest option. In addition, you may need to fix an extra nogging in the studwork to provide adequate support for the basin.

tools for the job

tape measure
cordless drill/driver
pipe cutter
adjustable spanners
panel saw
hammer
plastering or dry lining equipment

1 Check height measurements to be sure of the exact position of the basin and where brackets will need to be fixed to support it. Fix one or more extra noggings in place at the correct height for the brackets.

2 You may have to drill holes through studwork to provide for pipe rerouting.

3 Position the pipes and add appropriate connections as required (see pages 40–3).

4 Insert an insulation blanket between the studs. Nail a plasterboard sheet over the area, then dry line or plaster as required. Make access holes for the pipe tails to protrude into the room.

installing the basin

tools for the job

spirit level
tape measure
pencil
cordless drill/driver
and/or screwdriver
hacksaw
adjustable spanners

1 Draw a level pencil guideline where the brackets require fitting to correspond with the supporting points on the back of the basin. Screw the brackets directly into the wooden stud in hollow walls, or use wall plugs and screws in solid walls.

2 Attach the taps and waste pipe to the basin before hooking it in place over the supporting brackets. Screw the basin in place through the pre-drilled holes on its underside. Sometimes a plastic washer is supplied to produce a barrier between the screw and basin. Do not over-tighten the screw.

3 Hold the waste assembly in place and measure the length of pipe required to connect between the basin and trap. Cut the pipe to the appropriate length and make the necessary connections. You can now connect the taps to the hot and cold water supplies and the basin is ready for use.

Wall-mounted basins provide a compact and elegant finish. The chrome waste system matches the taps so that it does not detract from the decorative effect.

installing a bath ///

Before installing a bath, make sure that the necessary provision has been made for supply pipe and drainage pipe connections. In many cases, the existing pipework will be sufficient, but if the new bath is to be located in a different place from the old one, pipe adjustment will be required. Installation tends to be a two-part process. First, the feet and supportive framework is put in place, then the taps and drainage system are connected.

attaching the feet

Most baths have feet and supporting legs so that the underside of the bath is raised from the floor. The legs can be adjusted to take into account any unevenness across the floor surface. Most manufacturers supply baths without the feet attached.

1 Lay the bath upside down on a dust sheet to protect its surface. Most new baths are coated with a protective plastic film but this is really only meant for protecting against dirt and will not prevent scratches or scrapes. Position the bath legs in the sockets situated around the rim of the bath. These are generally secured in

the socket by a grub screw, which passes through the outside of the socket and into the leg.

2 Position the feet in the holes at the base of the legs using a nut on either side of the leg framework to hold them in place. Adjust the position of each foot to approximately the same height – these can be adjusted more accurately when the bath is in place. Most leg frames can also be screwed into the base of the bath through pre-drilled holes in the centre of the leg framework. Take care to use screws of the correct length so that they penetrate the chipboard base but not the bath itself.

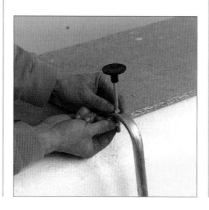

3 Most bath designs have a central leg to provide extra support. This is much smaller in size and is screwed, with a foot attached, in the middle of the bath base. Again, take care to use the correct length of screw.

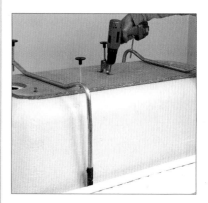

fitting & levelling

Once the legs and feet are attached, turn the bath right side up. Two people are needed for this because even very light baths are awkward to handle on your own. The next step is to fit the taps and waste pipes before finally levelling the bath once it is in position.

1 First attach the waste and overflow system to the bath. Pop-up waste designs for baths differ slightly from basins in that the waste is operated by a circular handle above the overflow outlet. A cable runs from the handle to the waste so that the plug hole can be opened and closed as required. Fit the supplied gaskets to both the waste outlet and overflow.

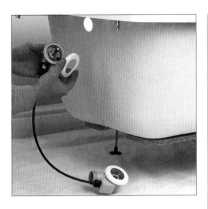

2 Holding one part of the waste outlet in one hand, screw the second part into the underside section through the outlet in the bath. Make sure that the appropriate gasket is positioned on this side of the outlet. If one is not supplied, apply a bead of silicone sealant instead.

3 Hold the back section of the overflow outlet in place in the same way, screwing the visible section of the assembly into position on the inside of the bath. Again, a gasket is generally supplied to create a watertight seal on this side of the assembly. Otherwise apply sealant.

4 Attach the overflow pipe between the overflow outlet and the underside of the waste assembly. Screw fitting collars with rubber washers are generally used for this.

5 Lower the taps through the pre-cut holes in the bath and secure them in place with a backnut. Most taps are seated on a gasket (as here) but, if one is not supplied, silicone sealant can be used instead.

6 Ease the bath towards its final position using a spirit level to help adjust leg heights to ensure that the bath is completely level.

7 The bath must be held securely in position. You can do this by cutting a channel in the wall and allowing the extreme edge of the bath to be supported in this channel. Alternatively, as shown here fix some supportive brackets into the wall and some corresponding brackets on the bath rim, then fit the rim over the brackets. Always double-check that the two halves of the brackets will align before screwing them in place.

8 Finally, connect the taps to the water supply and connect the drainage system (see pages 40–1), then screw the bath feet to the floor.

tips of the trade

It is important that baths are stable in order to avoid accidents. You can add extra support by inserting blocks of wood between the floor and underside of the bath. Weight can also be spread more efficiently if the feet are positioned on top of planks of wood. In many cases the extra height this produces is advantageous.

fitting a bath panel ⚡⚡

Traditional or roll-top baths did not usually have a bath panel, so the underside of the bath was always visible once installation was complete. However, most modern bathrooms employ some type of bath panel to box in the underside of the bathtub and so hide the framework and plumbing. This panelling can take the form of a permanent structure but it is always best to create a bath panel that can be easily removed for inspection purposes.

tools for the job

spirit level

pencil

tape measure

cordless drill/driver

panel saw or jigsaw

screwdriver

making a frame

In order to fit a panel, there must be a framework onto which it can be attached. For acrylic panels, this framework is normally integral. However, for more heavyweight alternatives such as wooden bath panels, wooden batten makes the ideal support.

1   Hold a spirit level vertically against the edge of the bath, allowing one end to touch the floor. Position a length of 5cm x 2.5cm (2in x 1in) batten on the floor parallel with the bath rim. Position a small block of wood (the same depth as the bath panel) between the bottom

of the spirit level and the batten. Move the spirit level and block along the edge of the bath and batten until the batten is in the precise position required for the base framework. Draw a pencil guideline along the edge of the batten.

2   Use the same method described in step 1 to work out the position for the base batten at the end of the bath. Again, mark the edge of the batten with a pencil guideline. Measure the distance between the walls and the intersection of the pencil guidelines and cut the battens accordingly.

3   Fix the longer batten in place. Cut a piece of 5cm x 5cm (2in x 2in) batten long enough to reach from the top of the base batten to the underside rim of the bath. Fix it at right angles to the shorter base batten. Fix the shorter base batten to the floor so that the thicker section of batten runs up under the rim of the bath at the corner for extra support. Alternatively, join two pieces of 5cm x 2.5cm (2in x 1in) batten together and use it for the same purpose.

4   Fix a batten to the wall at both the tap end of the bath and the opposite wall corner. These will be used as fixing points and support for the corresponding panel ends.

fitting the panel

With the framework in place, you can turn your attention to fitting the panel. Bath panels are generally supplied in standard sizes that must be cut down to meet your specific requirements.

1   Panels often need to be scribed so that they fit flush against both the walls and the skirting boards. Holding a small block of wood, cut

to the thickness of the base of the skirting, rest a pencil so that its point draws a guideline for cutting on the panel surface.

2 Cut along the pencil guideline with a panel saw or jigsaw. Choose a fine cutting blade so that the edges of the panel do not splinter.

3 Fix the main panel in place by screwing it into the batten framework. Do the same with the smaller end panel. Drill pilot holes through the end panel and into the edge of the main panel. Take care not to damage the surface of the panels.

4 Insert mirror screws into the pre-drilled holes to secure the panel.

5 Snap the covering cap on the screws to produce a neat finish.

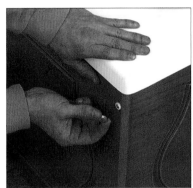

ALTERNATIVES TO WOODEN PANELLING

There are many different methods of panelling a bath in addition to the simple moulded wooden panel featured here. For example, a sheet of mdf (medium-density fibreboard) can be tiled and used as a bath panel. You will need to use a special tile drill bit to make pilot holes through the tiles, so that the screw fixings can be inserted through them to hold the panel in place on the framework. Another option is to attach sections of tongue and groove directly to a framework around the bath, although you will need to build inspection hatches into the design. Alternatively, the tongue and groove can be fixed to a sheet of mdf and used as a removable panel in the same way as the wooden one shown in the illustrated example. Yet another option for fixing the panel in place is to use magnetic catches instead of screw fixings.

Bath panels provide an attractive finishing feature and can be specifically chosen to complement the overall decorative scheme in the room.

fitting a toilet & cistern ⁄⁄⁄

A cursory glance at a toilet and cistern tends to suggest more complicated plumbing than is actually the case. Supply and drainage systems are in fact fairly simple and, as long as the toilet is not being moved too far from the original position, a changeover is a relatively straightforward process. Problems only tend to occur if soil pipes need lengthening or repositioning to accommodate a completely new toilet location.

close-coupled toilets

Most modern toilets follow a close-coupled design, whereby the cistern sits directly on top of the pan (see also page 27). This type of design is the easiest to fit and provides fewer complications than low-level or high-level toilets. The instructions provided here show the general principles involved in the fitting of a close-coupled design.

tools for the job

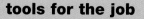

screwdriver

slip-joint pliers

1 First, assemble the internal cistern mechanism. Position the siphon unit inside the cistern by allowing the bottom threaded section to pass through the hole in the base of the cistern.

2 Fit the supplied rubber gasket over the threaded section, then position the connecting plate.

3 Secure the cistern connecting plate in position with a large threaded collar, then insert bolts in the holes on either side of the plate.

4 Insert the flushing mechanism or water control assembly into

the cistern, again allowing the threaded end of the water supply pipe to pass through the hole at the bottom of the cistern.

5 Secure it in place using the supplied washer/gasket and threaded collar. It is usually only necessary to tighten by hand the collars for the supply pipe and the siphon. Take care not to cross-thread either collar during the tightening process.

6 Fit the flushing handle to the cistern, holding it in place with a threaded collar. Make sure that the handle is linked to the flushing mechanism.

7 Ease the toilet pan into position, allowing the outlet pipe to marry with the soil pipe.

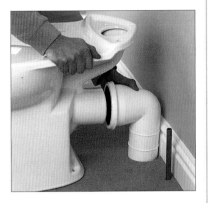

8 Lift the cistern onto the pan so that the connecting bolts thread through the retaining holes on the pan. Position a rubber gasket at the flush entrance so that the threaded section of the siphon unit is inserted through the gasket.

OTHER TYPES OF TOILET

• **Low-level toilets –** These have cisterns mounted on the wall above the pan, with a connecting pipe from the bottom of the cistern to the pan. The cistern must be attached to the wall with substantial fixings because, unlike a close-coupled toilet, the pan does not support any of its weight.

• **High-level toilets –** The cistern is fitted high up the wall so the flush pipe needs to be much longer. Again, wall fixings must be sturdy enough to support the cistern weight.

9 Fit the nuts supplied by the manufacturer to the cistern connecting bolts using both rubber and metal washers to hold the cistern securely in place. This will provide a barrier between the metal and ceramic surfaces.

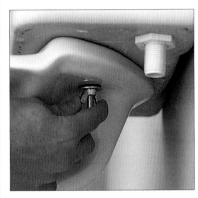

10 Connect the supply pipe for the cold water supply to the cistern using slip-joint pliers.

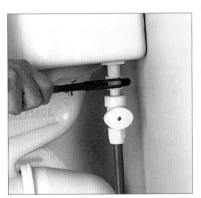

11 If the cistern has pre-drilled holes in its back, next to the wall, insert screws to secure the cistern in place. Again, use both metal and rubber washers.

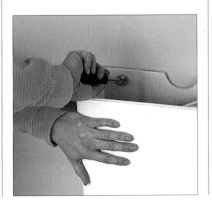

You should also insert retaining screws through the holes at the base of the pan in order to hold it securely in position.

12 Finally, fit the toilet seat by securing it in place through the pre-drilled holes at the back of the pan. Turn the water supply back on – the toilet is now ready for use.

REPOSITIONING A TOILET AGAINST AN INTERIOR WALL

Complications will occur if a toilet is to be moved from an exterior wall to an interior one. The reason that toilets are usually located on or close to an exterior wall is because there is easy access to the soil pipe, which tends to run down exterior walls and into the sewer system. Having the toilet on an interior wall necessitates extending the large drainage pipe from the toilet out to the soil pipe. Clearly, the dimensions of the drainage pipe make routing difficult because it is unlikely to fit and have the required run if it is positioned below floor level. The alternative method of running the pipe around interior walls is unsightly and is also unlikely to provide the necessary run. As a result, keeping the new toilet position close to the existing one or at least situated on an external wall will always make fitting procedures much easier.

installing a bidet ⌁⌁⌁

If you have the luxury of a spacious bathroom, a bidet is a very useful fitting. There are two types: over-rim and rim supply. The former is illustrated here and has water coming from taps above the bidet rim. A rim supply bidet fills from below the rim and as such warms the seat as water is pumped into the bowl. This system has a risk of back siphonage, which means a dedicated hot and cold water supply is essential, making it a more complicated undertaking.

over-rim supply bidets

In many ways an over-rim supply bidet is installed in a similar way to a bathroom basin. First, make sure that both hot and cold water supplies have been routed for bidet connection (see pages 40-3). The waste pipe can be joined directly to the soil pipe or connected to the basin or bath waste pipe. A simple T-connector can be cut into either one of these waste outlets for this purpose. However, consider waste heights carefully because there can be a danger of water from a basin running back into the pan of the bidet if the waste is much higher than the bidet. Also, waste from the bidet could run back into the bath if it is much higher than the bath waste. You need to adjust the run of waste pipes to account for such potential problems.

tools for the job

slip-joint pliers
adjustable spanners
screwdriver
tape measure
pipe cutter

1 Thread the top section of the pop-up waste outlet through the outlet in the bidet, making sure that the correct gasket has been fitted over the tail. If a gasket is not supplied with the outlet, it can be seated on a layer of silicone sealant

to produce the necessary watertight seal. If using sealant, be sure to wipe away the excess before it has a chance to dry.

2 Screw the bottom section of the waste onto the top section underneath the bidet. Again, make sure that the correct gasket is positioned between the waste section and the ceramic surface of the bidet.

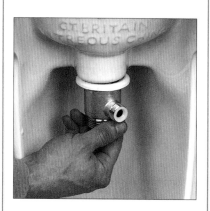

3 Turn your attention to the monobloc tap for the bidet. Position a sealing washer at the base of the tap – again, if the taps you are using are not supplied with sealing washers, they can be seated on silicone sealant.

4 Fit the copper hot and cold water supply pipes to the base of the tap fitting, screwing them firmly in place, but taking care not to over-tighten them. Fit the threaded bolt that will be used to secure the tap in position.

5 Thread the copper pipes of the tap assembly through the hole in the bidet. Secure the tap assembly in place using the supplied washers or backnuts. Fit a locking nut onto the threaded bolt, tightening by hand. You may have to give the nut one or two turns with an adjustable spanner to ensure the taps are securely in place. Take care not to over-tighten.

8 Make sure that all the necessary supply pipes and waste pipes are in place, ready for the bidet to be positioned and connected. In this case, a swept T-connector has been used to make the appropriate connection in an existing waste pipe. Shut-off valves have also been fitted to the supply pipes so that water can be turned off in an emergency. See pages 40-3.

9 Position the bidet, connecting the supply pipes and waste outlet and trap. Secure the bidet in place by inserting screws at the base of the bidet through the pre-drilled holes. Take care not to over-tighten these fixings and use washers if supplied by the manufacturer. The water supply may now be turned on and the bidet used.

6 Screw the pop-up waste lever into the base of the waste outlet. Tightening by hand is usually sufficient, although you may need to use adjustable spanners.

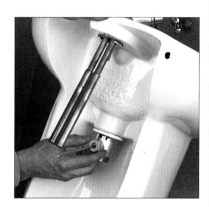

7 Insert the pop-up waste rod into the waste lever and join it to the lever with the supplied clamp. Fix them in place, using a screwdriver to tighten the connection. Adjust the fixing if necessary so that the waste bung sits correctly in the outlet. The pop-up waste bung itself is also adjustable to ensure a watertight fit in the outlet, so make any necessary adjustments now.

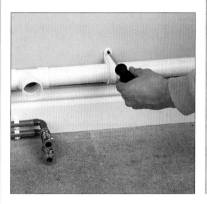

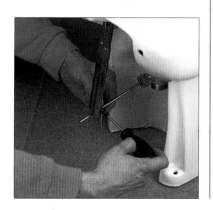

Providing an extra dimension of hygiene and comfort, bidets can also be a highly ornate element of a bathroom design.

installing a shower ⁄⁄⁄⁄

Showers are convenient and efficient bathroom fittings that consume a fraction of the water used by baths. Shower types vary, as do the mechanisms by which they are controlled (see pages 30–1) – our main concern here is the installation procedure. A shower that is sunk into a wall tends to create a more aesthetically pleasing finish, but surface mounting the shower is generally easier to implement. In this example, a shower unit is being fitted into a stud wall.

recessed shower units

tools for the job

tape measure

cordless drill/driver

slip-joint pliers

adjustable spanners

plasterboarding & tiling equipment

1 You will need to install an extra nogging inside the wall to act as a mounting position for the shower. If it is a new wall, do this during the construction process. If it is an existing wall, strip the plasterboard and fix a nogging at the required height and at a depth that will allow the shower unit to sit behind the wall surface, with the controls protruding beyond it. Route hot and cold water supply pipes to the correct position in the wall.

2 Secure the shower unit in place on the supporting nogging so that the connections for the water supply marry with the unit. Cut the

pipe length with a pipe cutter if necessary. Use an adjustable spanner to tighten the connections between the supply pipes and shower unit.

3 In many cases you will need to connect an additional length of pipe from the unit to the shower head. Follow the guidelines provided by the manufacturer.

4 You should now complete the wall. Marine plywood makes a good background for a tiled shower enclosure, but plasterboard can be used as long as it is sealed and/or plastered. Screw the decorative part of the shower head supply pipe onto the recessed part of the pipe.

5 Fit the appropriate collars and/or washers over the unit and supply pipe. These generally push into place.

6 Fit the shower head retaining bracket on the wall and connect the hose to the supply pipe.

installing a bath screen

If a shower is being installed above a bath, you must fit a bath screen to protect the room from water spray.

tools for the job

tape measure
spirit level
cordless drill/driver
screwdriver

1 Use a spirit level to fix the channelling for the frame vertically above the edge of the bath. If fixing into tiles, use the correct type of drill bit to make pilot holes so that you do not damage the tiled surface.

2 Fix the hinging mechanism to the channelling. Designs vary but in many cases the hinge is a two-part assembly. The first part is used to create a secure wall fixing, to which a second section is added.

3 Fit the corresponding hinge sections onto the screen. These are normally of a decorative design. Take care to place any gaskets or protective barriers between the metallic part of the hinge and, in this case, the glass surface.

4 Here, a retaining bolt is pushed through the hinge barrel. It holds the door in place while allowing the hinging mechanism to push the door backwards and forwards from the bath edge. Fit rubber sealant strips to the under edge of the screen.

Simple bath screens provide a physical barrier that prevents water overspray. Different shapes and designs can be chosen to match your bathroom layout.

installing a shower cubicle

If room allows, it is always more convenient to have a shower separate from the bath. In this case, you will need to build a shower cubicle to contain overspray. Shower cubicles also require a tray to act as the collecting area for water, and a drainage outlet needs to be positioned to carry away the waste. When starting from scratch, make sure that drainage pipes have been routed to the shower position and that supply pipes are also in place.

installing the tray

Most shower cubicles are fitted in the corner of a room and are composed of two screen walls and a square shower tray. The basic technique for installation remains the same no matter what the cubicle shape.

tools for the job

tape measure & pencil
jigsaw
cordless drill/driver
bucket
pointing or gauging trowel
spirit level

1 Position the shower tray 'dry', then cut out a section of the hardboard subfloor through which drainage pipes may be installed. Make sure there is space for an access hatch on the outside edge of the shower tray. Nail batten underneath the edges of the hatch hole, then cut a piece of hardboard to fit and position it on top of the batten.

2 Fit the waste outlet in the shower tray. Make sure that gaskets or washers are fitted on both sides of the waste opening to ensure that a watertight seal is made around the edge of the outlet.

3 Mix some mortar into a firm consistency (4 parts building sand to 1 part cement) and spread it in sections on the floor area where the tray is to be positioned.

4 Position the tray, allowing it to bed down into the mortar. Place a spirit level across all angles on the tray to make sure that it is perfectly level. If necessary, remove the tray and adjust the mortar beneath.

5 Connect the trap to the waste outlet and join it to the waste outlet pipe. Shower traps are designed so that they are as shallow as possible – a deep trap makes it more difficult to provide room, or height, for a good run on the outlet pipe.

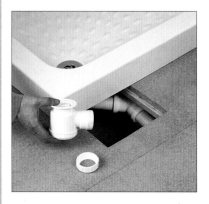

tips of the trade

Having enough room for the drainage pipe to run under a shower is often a problem, so it can be helpful to install the tray slightly higher than floor level. Many showers do in fact have a step up to them for this reason, so always bear in mind drainage requirements when choosing and installing a tray.

installing the cubicle

The door designs for shower cubicles vary considerably. The hinged design, shown here, is very common and is the best example to illustrate installation procedures.

tools for the job

tape measure

pencil

spirit level

cordless drill/driver

screwdriver

1 Specially designed channels are used to hold the sections of the cubicle on the wall. Position them perfectly vertical on the edges of the tray. They usually sit centrally on the edge of the tray.

2 Fix the channels to the wall above the two corners of the tray using the appropriate fixings.

3 Slot the non-opening screen section of the cubicle into one of the wall channels. Position the opening section in the other channel and hold both in place so that they meet at the required point on the corner of the tray (it is a good idea for someone else to help with this).

4 Fix the cubicle sections in place by drilling pilot holes through the wall channels and into the frame, with self-tapping screws to hold them in place. Choose drill bits so that the pilot holes are smaller than the screws.

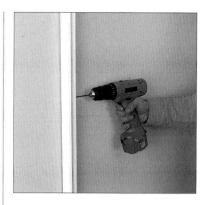

5 Attach a handle to the door then apply silicone sealant around the internal edges and between all joints.

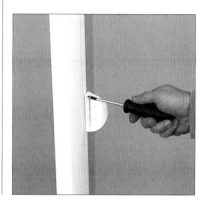

Once the shower unit is installed and the cubicle tiled, this practical bathroom fixture can make an excellent feature in the overall bathroom design.

boxing in ⤢

Bathrooms that are based on a fitted design, and therefore incorporate many units in their layout, do not usually require much boxing in because the units themselves hide most of the pipework. However, where bathroom design is based around the actual fittings without any custom-made units, it is a good idea to box in the more unsightly areas of pipes and connections in order to provide a more aesthetically pleasing finish.

simple boxing

There are several types of building board that can be used for boxing, but cut sections of mdf (medium-density fibreboard) attached to a framework of 5 x 2.5cm (2 x 1in) battens provides the best arrangement to cope with most boxing-in needs.

The secret of good boxing in is to keep its design as simple as possible. This uses resources efficiently and means that you can finish what can be a slightly tedious task as quickly as possible. The standard of finish to which you make the boxing will depend on the final decoration that will be applied to it. If you are simply going to paint it, then you must make sure that joints and fixings are as neat as possible. If it is to be tiled, however, then making accurate joints is not so essential since any small defects will be covered by the tiles.

tools for the job

tape measure & pencil
cordless drill/driver
spirit level
jigsaw
hammer
punch

1 The precise position of the battens will depend on the items to be boxed in. At floor level, fix a batten as close to the wall or skirting board as possible, but make sure that when mdf is applied to the framework it will clear the pipes it is trying to cover. Boxing should protrude into the room as small a distance as possible, while still effectively covering up pipework and other obstacles.

2 Attach wall battens directly above pipework. Make sure that the batten is fixed precisely level and held securely in place.

3 In many cases mdf can be fitted easily by simply measuring dimension requirements. However, if you have to accommodate obstacles such as basin pedestals, scribe mdf edges in order to gain as precise a fit as possible.

4 Once cut to size, nail or screw the front section of mdf in place.

5 Fix the top section to the front section along the right-angled joint made by the two pieces. Punch in the nail heads below surface level.

In many cases you will need to provide a hatch in the boxing design to allow access to items such as basin traps and shut-off valves.

tools for the job

tape measure
pencil
jigsaw
cordless drill/driver
hammer
punch
screwdriver

1 Cut mdf to the size required for the boxing. Use a template such as a standard wall tile to draw a guideline on the mdf for the hatch.

2 Cut out a hole in the mdf with a jigsaw and position two small blocks on either edge of the hole on what will be the inside of the boxing.

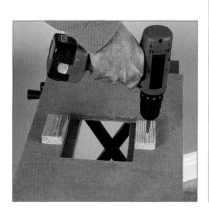

3 Clamp the mdf vertically in a workbench and secure magnetic catches to the edges of the wooden blocks fixed in step 2.

4 Cut a piece of mdf to the same size as the hole – this will be the hatch – and fit the second half or plate of each magnetic catch to the corresponding positions on the hatch. Fit a small handle on the centre of the hatch and put the hatch in place.

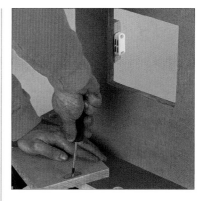

HATCH OPTIONS

• **Hinges –** Use piano hinges instead of magnetic catches to create a hinged hatch mechanism.

• **Large sections –** In some cases it is best to make an entire section of boxing removable. Hold the section in place with a few screws, which can then be removed if access is required.

Here the boxing hides away the pipework behind the toilet, neatening the overall finish of the bathroom and forming a handy shelf at the same time.

fitting bathroom accessories

Once all the main bathroom fittings are in place, you can turn your attention to the accessories that complement them. Mirrors, cabinets and towel rails are all items that serve both a functional and decorative purpose. They must therefore be fixed in place correctly if they are to fulfil both these roles. This chapter considers a range of bathroom accessories and the ways in which they can be incorporated into your chosen bathroom design.

65

The main accessories in this bathroom are a pair of mirrors, which give the illusion of space, and a stylish towel rail.

accessory options

Accessories form a huge segment of the bathroom design market, and manufacturing innovations make this an exciting area of home improvement. Most people are no longer satisfied with standard bathroom layouts and instead require a design with extra practical and decorative features. Manufacturers have recognized this change of attitude and now produce a wide range of extra features that can help create the required atmosphere.

shelving

Shelves are found in many rooms in the home and the bathroom is no exception. The design of the shelving should complement the general decoration of the room, and a simple single shelf can offer just as much visual impact as a larger storage system. Bathroom shelves are often as much for display purposes as for more practical needs such as housing toiletries. In fact, the many luxurious bathing products now available are usually so beautifully packaged that they look wonderful when displayed on a shelf. Also remember that room features such as a window sill can be tiled to create an attractive shelf.

RIGHT *This simple, elegant glass shelf with chrome supporting brackets provides a useful storage surface that is also ideal for displaying ornaments and flowers.*

mobile storage

Not all shelves or cupboards have to be fixed in place. Chests and tables in other rooms in the home are often moveable, and there is no reason why this cannot be the case in the bathroom. This type of storage system is generally smaller than fixed storage so that it is not too cumbersome to move, but its flexibility means that you can experiment with different layout options. Mobile storage can be unsuitable for bathrooms with limited floor space.

LEFT *This shaving mirror and shelf are an excellent example of a small but compact unit that can be moved to other areas of the bathroom when not in use.*

heated towel rails

Although heated towel rails have been available for many years, recently the number of different styles available has expanded immensely. Gone are the days of draping towels over radiators – these custom-designed rails now fulfil the dual-purpose role of heating the bathroom as well as keeping towels dry. Electrically operated and water-heated rails are available making it even easier to choose the right one for your personal needs.

mirrors

It is rare to find a bathroom without at least one mirror. This essential grooming accessory can be fixed permanently to walls or hung like a picture and frame. As well as having a practical function, mirrors are also ideal for making small bathrooms appear larger, especially if the mirror takes up a large proportion of a wall surface.

ABOVE RIGHT *Modern towel rails possess a certain elegance and flair that was often missing from older models.*

RIGHT *Bathroom manufacturers increasingly tailor mirror design to complement the finish and style of the other fittings and fixtures they produce.*

BELOW *As with many bathroom accessories, cabinets can be purchased as part of a larger set of items. Here, the cabinet, bathroom shelf and towel rail combine to create a 'ship' theme, helping to produce a harmonious overall appearance.*

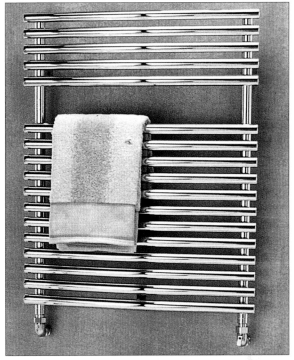

cabinets

Cabinets or bathroom cupboards are generally essential items. They allow large quantities of items to be stored and enable you to keep potentially harmful medicine out of reach of children. Sometimes they are fronted with a mirror and therefore perform a dual function, but their main purpose is to provide effective storage.

fitting a heated towel rail ⁄⁄⁄

It is currently popular to remove bathroom radiators and install heated towel rails. These keep towels dry and heat the room, either by electricity or water. Replacing a radiator with a water-heated towel rail is generally a straightforward procedure since the water supply is already in place and will require only minor changes for connecting it to the rail. If you wish to position the rail in a different location, however, you will have to reroute the supply pipes.

water-heated towel rails

tools for the job

long-nose pliers
adjustable spanners
tape measure
pencil
spirit level
cordless drill/driver
screwdriver
slip-joint pliers

safety advice

Electrically operated towel rails need an electrical supply and this should be routed and connected by a qualified electrician. As with all electrical work in the bathroom, there are strict regulations and, therefore, this job should be left to the professionals.

1 Use a pair of long-nose pliers to remove the plastic bungs from the ends of the rail (these protect the threads for valves).

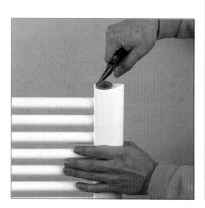

2 Hand screw a blanking plug in one top corner of the rail and a ventilation or bleed valve in the other.

3 Once the threads are correctly engaged, carefully tighten both the plug and the valve using an adjustable spanner.

tips of the trade

To prevent the surface of plugs or valves from being scratched by the spanners, wrap masking tape around the spanner jaws to soften their sharp edges. This is particularly important if the plugs or valves play a decorative role in the finished look of the rail.

4 Screw in the valves at the bottom of the rail by hand before tightening with a spanner.

5 Decide on the required height for the towel rail – it is usually positioned so that the bottom of the rail is slightly above or level with the top of the skirting board. Use a spirit level to draw a horizontal guideline on the wall to help you position the top two retaining brackets. They usually sit between the horizontal tubular sections of the rail, slightly down from the top of the rail. Using appropriate fixings, depending on whether the wall is solid or hollow, fix the first pieces of the bracket assemblies in place.

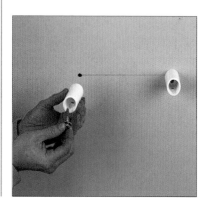

6 Measure the position of the bottom bracket or brackets. When there is only one, it should be positioned central to the rail and up slightly from its bottom edge. Insert the second part of the bracket assemblies into the fixed sections.

7 The bracket assemblies are made in this way so that they can be adjusted slightly once the rail is in place.

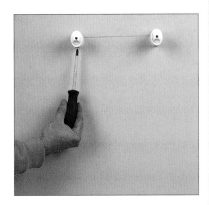

8 Position the rail on the brackets and use the next part of the bracket assemblies to secure the rail in place.

9 Cover the fixings of the brackets with the supplied clip-on caps in order to produce a neat finish.

10 Connect the valves to the supply pipes. In this case, the pipes have been routed under the floor to the rail position after it was installed. This ensures that the rail is perfectly level before connection. Pipes can be brought into position before fixing the rail but, unless measurements are precise, you may have to make awkward adjustments to the pipe lengths and connections. This type of plumbing is best left to the professionals.

tips of the trade

If the rail is supplied with a protective covering, leave this on until it is fixed in place on the wall. Although you will have to make holes in the covering to fix the brackets, it is best to leave the rest in place to protect against scratches and scrapes during the fitting procedure.

A slimline design combined with neat installation make heated towel rails an ideal dual-purpose fitting for any bathroom.

installing ventilation ⚑⚑⚑

Ventilation is important in bathrooms because of their damp, moist atmosphere. This type of environment suffers from condensation, which can damage decoration and finishes unless adequate ventilation systems are installed. The advent of double-glazing has increased the problem and made ventilation systems essential since the somewhat draughty nature of older windows and doors did at least allow some flow of air.

mechanical ventilation

Mechanical ventilation is usually in the form of extractor fans. These fittings remove the damp air from the room and help to produce a less humid atmosphere. They can be positioned in either walls or ceilings. The latter is particularly common in shower cubicles. Most are operated by an electrical supply that switches the fan on automatically when the light is turned on in the room. This mode of operation varies according to the manufacturer, and many designs incorporate automatic cut-off switches after a set period of time. It is worth bearing in mind that building regulations in new properties specify that an extractor fan must be fitted in a bathroom.

WALL-MOUNTED FAN

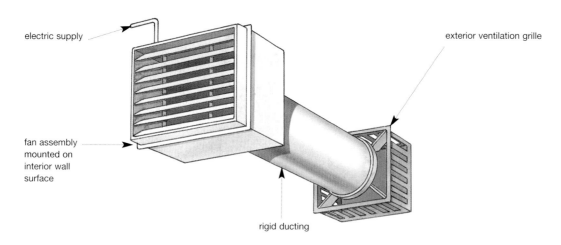

electric supply

exterior ventilation grille

fan assembly mounted on interior wall surface

rigid ducting

CEILING-MOUNTED FAN

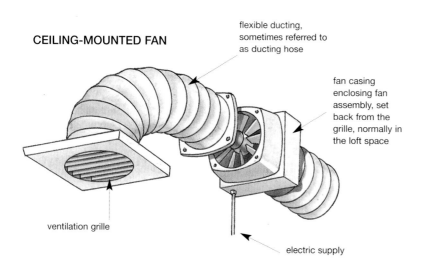

flexible ducting, sometimes referred to as ducting hose

fan casing enclosing fan assembly, set back from the grille, normally in the loft space

ventilation grille

electric supply

WINDOW-MOUNTED FANS

Fans that can be fixed into a circular hole in a windowpane are readily available. You will need to cut the hole using the correct type of glass cutter, although it may be easier to get your local glass merchant to perform this task. You should never attempt cutting holes in double-glazed windows. The actual fan assembly is fitted on the inside of the pane, with an inner casing covering the moving parts. An exterior grille is used to finish the outer part of the assembly.

For wall-mounted fans, a hole must be cut through the wall to the exterior of the house. In order to cut a hole through masonry with any degree of accuracy, you will need to hire a core drill bit and drill. It is not worth buying this type of equipment because it is extremely expensive and will only be needed for very occasional use – it is much more cost effective to hire from a local supplier. For ceiling-mounted fans, the equipment required is not as heavy duty since there is no masonry work involved. The simple technique for making an access hole in a plaster ceiling is demonstrated here.

tools for the job

pencil & tape measure
pipe, cable & joist detector
padsaw
screwdriver

1 Work out the position of the fan, using a cable, pipe and joist detector to check that there are no supply pipes or cables in this area. These will obstruct the fan and could be dangerous if cut. There should also be no ceiling joists because they would make it impossible to install the fan. You may, therefore, have to make a small compromise when deciding on a position. Hold the grille in place on the ceiling and use a pencil to draw around the circumference of the circular section of the grille. This provides a cutting guideline.

2 When you have determined the the the position of the fan, use a padsaw or dry wall saw to cut out the circular section of ceiling.

3 Secure the first part of the grille assembly in the hole with retaining screws. Clip the grille in place, then fit the ducting hose and extractor above the grille assembly.

Static vents are an alternative type of bathroom ventilation that do not involve any mechanical parts. They simply allow air to flow in the room, using natural draughts to create the circulation. Some examples of static vent systems, and covers that are used to neaten the finished look, are shown here.

Louvre vents act as the interior covers for ventilation holes or ducts in exterior walls. Different designs and finishes are available. Plastic and aluminium examples are shown here. Plastic vents can be painted to blend with wall finishes. As with the air brick, the grille is permanently open.

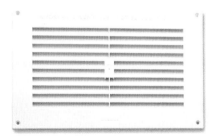

Hit-and-miss vents are interior covers for holes or ducts that have an opening and closing mechanism.

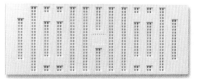

Air bricks are positioned in the wall structure and are permanently open.

fitting shelving ✂

Shelving provides simple, effective storage and display areas. Although boxed or panelled areas around bathtubs create ledges that can act as additional shelving, most bathrooms also have independent shelving systems fixed to wall surfaces. There are many designs available – examples of two types of shelving wall bracket system are shown here. A technique is also shown for converting a windowsill into a tiled shelf.

hidden-fixings brackets

Some bracket designs allow you to hide the fixings, which will improve the general appearance once the shelving is in use. Manufacturers are always making innovations in this area to maximize the decorative as well as functional aspects of shelving.

tools for the job

tape measure
pencil
mini level
bradawl
hammer
cordless drill/driver
spirit level

1 Mark off with a pencil the position of the shelf on the wall. Hold the housing section of one bracket against the wall and position it using a mini level to ensure it is precisely vertical. Use a bradawl to mark the fixing position.

2 Drill the required size holes in the wall and fit wall plugs into them. You may be able to push them in by hand – if not, tap them once or twice with the butt end of a hammer.

3 Reposition the housing section and screw it in place. Check it with a mini level to make sure it has not shifted out of position.

4 Position the other housing section on the wall next to the fixed one at the distance required to accommodate the shelf. Place a spirit level across the top of both sections to ensure that they are precisely level and aligned. Use a bradawl to mark the screw position.

5 Fix the second section in place and slide the support brackets into both the housing sections.

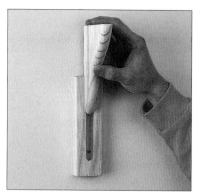

6 Position the shelf and secure it with panel pins through the top of the shelf into the brackets below.

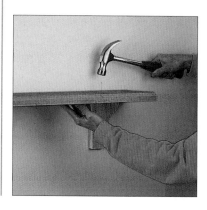

Where bracket fixings are visible, you will need to fill fixing holes before the shelf is decorated in order to produce the best possible finished look.

tools for the job

tape measure & pencil
cordless drill/driver
mini level
bradawl
spirit level
hammer

1 Mark shelf position and then secure the first bracket in place with appropriate fixings. Use a mini level to ensure it is vertical.

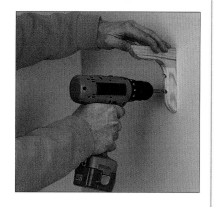

2 Use a bradawl to mark the required fixing points for the second bracket. Use a mini level to check it is vertical and a spirit level to ensure that both brackets are level.

3 Screw the second bracket in place, then hammer panel pins or small nails to hold the shelf in position, fixing through the top of the shelf and into the brackets below. Screw some hooks to the underside of the shelf as extra storage.

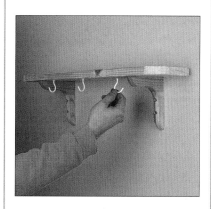

tiling a windowsill

You can create some shelving from existing features in the room. For example, a tiled windowsill makes an ideal bathroom shelf.

tools for the job

notched spreader
tape measure
mini hacksaw
tile cutting machine
grout spreader
sponge

1 Use a notched spreader to apply tile adhesive to the windowsill.

2 Cut an edging strip to the appropriate size and position it in the adhesive along the front edge of the window-sill.

3 Centralize the tile design by positioning the first full tile in the middle of the windowsill at its front edge. Slip the edge of the tile under the edging strip.

4 Continue to add full tiles, positioning any cut tiles last. See pages 100-3 for more information on laying tiles. Once the window-sill is complete, allow the adhesive to dry before grouting all the tile joints.

fitting cabinets ↗

Most bathrooms have at least one cabinet that is used for storing toiletries and/or medicines. Many fulfil an additional function by having a mirror on the door of the cabinet, hence the ideal location for installing such a cabinet is above a basin. If a bathroom cabinet is to be used for storing medicines, make sure it is positioned out of the reach of children or has a locking mechanism so that you can control access.

cabinet design

Along with all bathroom accessories, there is a wide choice of cabinet designs. As well as size differences, they are available in numerous finishes. Many cabinets have open storage areas which are ideal for storing items that are in everyday use, so that you do not have to keep opening and closing the cabinet.

single door mirror cabinet
with shelf

corner cabinet

double door mirror cabinet
with shelf

single door
mirror cabinet

double door cabinet with
colourwash effect

ornamental
antique cabinet

PAINTING CABINETS

Many cabinets are supplied varnished or stained, but there is nothing to stop you from painting the cabinet to match other decorations in the room. Simply sand back the wooden surface thoroughly, then prime it and apply your chosen paint finish.

fixing in position

Even lightweight cabinets will put a considerable strain on the wall fixings once they are filled with toiletries and the like, so all cabinets must be fixed securely to ensure there is no danger of their falling off the wall. Most cabinets are supplied with fixings and instructions, and the example shown here demonstrates a typical technique for securing a cabinet in place. When positioning a cabinet, it is always best to have a helper so that one person can hold the cabinet roughly in place while the other checks it for height suitability. This is especially important if the door(s) of the cabinet include a mirror, because it will need to be positioned at a height that is ideal for all members of the household.

tools for the job

tape measure

pencil

spirit level

cordless drill/driver

screwdriver

1 This cabinet has pre-drilled holes in the back, so it is necessary to measure the distance between the holes as accurately as possible. There are two holes near the top of the cabinet and two near the bottom. You need to measure the distance between the holes from side to side and from top to bottom.

2 Transfer these measurements onto the wall using a spirit level to draw horizontal lines representing the distances between the holes. Mark the required hole positions on the lines, then drill and insert wall plugs at these points.

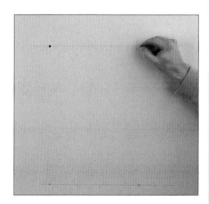

3 Hold the cabinet in position and screw through the inside into the wall plug fixings. In this case, fixing blocks have been supplied to add greater strength to the fixings. A hand-held screwdriver has been used here because it can be difficult to gain access to the corners of the cabinet using a cordless drill. Shelving may or may not be fixed in place in the cabinet at the time of

manufacture. If it is not, tap the supporting brackets for the shelves into the sides of the cabinet at the appropriate positions, then slide the shelves into place.

4 Attach handles if required, screwing them through the pre-drilled holes on the doors.

If the holes for handles have not been pre-drilled at the manufacturing stage, use a cordless drill and an appropriate size drill bit to make pilot holes. Hold a block of wood on the other side of the door so that the drill bit goes into the block when it emerges and does not cause the door surface to splinter.

Cabinets fulfil an important bathroom function by providing essential storage and also act as interesting features on open wall surfaces.

fitting mirrors ↗↗

Mirrors are an integral part of bathroom layout and there is a wide range to choose from, both in terms of design and the methods by which they are fixed to wall surfaces. The main problem when installing mirrors is that it is not possible to fix through them unless pre-drilled holes have been made at the time of manufacture. Specially designed brackets or adhesive must be used instead to hold the mirror in place on the wall.

heated mirrors

tools for the job

pencil

tape measure

spirit level

cordless drill/driver

1 In this example the mirror is positioned above a splashback using flush fixings screwed into the wall. Begin by marking the fixing points for the two lower clips by drawing a level line on the wall using a spirit level. Here, the line is drawn above the splashback because the recesses into which the clips will insert are set back slightly from the edge of the mirror on its reverse side.

2 Fix the two bottom clips in place on the drawn guideline, making sure that their distance apart corresponds with the distance between the insertion points on the back of the mirror.

3 Measure upwards from the two bottom clips to mark the position for the top two. Again, make sure that their distance apart corresponds with that of the insertion points on the back of the mirror. It is a good idea to draw a vertical line upwards from the lower clips to mark the position of the top ones, in which case you should use a spirit level to ensure accuracy.

4 Screw the top two clips in place. These have a slightly different design from the lower ones, in that they have an elongated oval-shaped hole for the screw fixing rather than a round hole. This is so

that they can slide up and down on the screw fixing. Insert the screw through the bottom of the oval.

safety advice

Do not attempt to carry out electrical wiring and connection yourself. This must always be done by an electrician.

5 Once the wiring is complete, position the mirror on the wall surface. Fit the bottom edge of the mirror into the lower clips, then lay the mirror flat against the wall and slide the top clips down into the insertion points on the back of it.

using adhesive

Another way of fixing a mirror to a wall surface is to use mirror adhesive or a strong bonding adhesive. These are available in tubes and are expelled with the aid of a sealant gun. You will need to support the weight of the mirror while the adhesive dries.

tools for the job

tape measure & pencil

panel saw

mini level

cordless drill/driver

sealant gun or dispenser

1 Cut a length of batten equal to the width of the mirror. Fix it to the wall at the position where the base of the mirror will be. Use a mini level to check that the batten is level.

2 Apply adhesive generously to the back of the mirror.

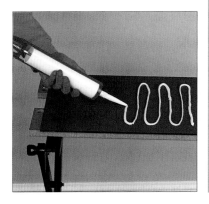

3 Position the mirror with its bottom edge on top of the batten. Once the adhesive has dried, remove the batten, fill the screw holes with filler and decorate the wall.

mirror tiles

tools for the job

pencil

tape measure

spirit level

1 Use a spirit level to draw a pencil guideline on the wall at the point where the bottom edge of the first row of tiles will sit. Draw a vertical guideline to help you position the first column of tiles precisely. Attach self-adhesive pads to the backs of the tiles. One on each corner is usually sufficient, but you should read the manufacturer's guidelines because some heavier or larger tiles may need more pads to support them.

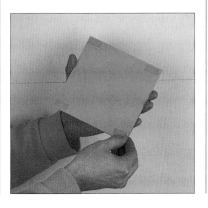

2 Use the pencil guideline you have drawn to position the tiles on the wall, gradually building up your chosen design. In most cases you can butt the tile edges up against each other, although some manufacturers may recommend leaving a small gap.

MIRROR SCREWS

Mirror screws are the best option for fixing mirrors with pre-drilled holes in their surface. The screws are specially designed so that decorative caps can be fixed over the screw head once the mirror is in place. Like many fixings, different manufacturers produce different designs, so you are likely to find variations in the types of mirror screw available. Some designs include a rubber grommet that should be positioned in the mirror hole before the screw is inserted. This helps to minimize the risk of the mirror cracking when the screw comes into contact with the edge of the hole (although you still need to be careful when inserting the screw to make sure that you do not over-tighten it). In the same way that screw designs vary, so do the actual caps that fit over the screw heads. Designs range from rounded domes to more flattened, squarer shapes. Some caps actually screw in place onto the mirror screw, while others are snapped or clipped in position like a popper fastening.

flooring

Although floor space is often restricted in a bathroom compared with other rooms in the home, choosing the most suitable finish to cater for your needs still requires careful consideration. Some floor coverings are not ideal for bathroom use because of the damp conditions – carpets, for example, can retain moisture too easily, leading to rapid decay. Materials that can be cleaned or wiped easily, such as tiles or vinyl, are preferable. This chapter looks at popular choices of flooring for bathrooms and demonstrates the best techniques for laying and finishing them.

A decorative pattern has been created for the floor in this bathroom using hard tiles of different sizes and colour.

flooring options

Appearance, texture and comfort are all equally important factors when considering flooring. The bathroom is an area of the home where a lot of time can be spent barefoot, so achieving a certain level of underfoot comfort is essential. Some people will accept the cold feel of a hard tiled floor because they prefer the durability and aesthetic quality of this type of flooring whereas others may opt for cushioned vinyl, which provides a slightly warmer and more comfortable feel.

hard tiles

The different types of hard tiles available varies enormously in terms of quality and price. Tiles can be bought glazed or unglazed, and the techniques for laying them may have to be modified slightly according to the characteristics of the particular tile you choose. Whatever type you decide on, however, hard tiles are an ideal bathroom flooring option and provide an exceptionally durable finish, although they are the most difficult type of flooring to lay. If you have a particular aversion to the cold feel of hard tiles underfoot, it is possible to install underfloor heating mechanisms beneath the hard tile finish.

RIGHT *Tile designs can be kept simple, or a slightly more individual look can be achieved by varying tile size and colour to produce a more decorative pattern.*

wooden floorboards

Wooden floorboards can provide a suitable bathroom floor covering, as long as they are treated and finished in the correct manner with either paint, stain, and/or varnish to seal their surface so that water cannot penetrate. You will need to put a certain amount of work into preparing their surface to make sure that it is acceptable underfoot, but the finished results are worthwhile. There is also the option of removing old floorboards that have been damaged beyond repair and laying new ones in their place. Although there will be extra expense in this procedure, you will save time and money otherwise spent in the preparation of older boards. Consider using tongue and groove floorboards so that there will be no visible fixings through the top surface of the boards, which will lead to a more pleasing finish.

LEFT *Floorboards produce a wonderfully natural look in a bathroom. Pale stains or varnishes are often the best choice to show off the natural grain of the wood. The battens framing the walls continue the wooden theme in this room and help to accentuate its weather-beaten, seaside ambience.*

laminate floors

Although laminate floors have been used in most rooms in the home for some time, they used to be deemed unsuitable for bathroom use. However, many manufacturers now produce designs that will stand up to the rigours of a damp atmosphere. Always check with the manufacturer that the flooring you choose is suitable for bathroom use before purchase.

cork tiles

Cork tiles are an excellent choice for bathrooms because they are comfortable underfoot and easily cleaned. They are also relatively easy to lay compared with other types of tiles. In the past they were only available in a natural brown or buff finish, but it is now possible to buy coloured varieties, which gives many more options in terms of building up patterns and designs

ABOVE RIGHT *Smooth to the touch and highly decorative in appearance, laminate floors are becoming increasingly popular in bathrooms.*

RIGHT *Cork's natural finish provides an attractive and practical floor covering that is comfortable underfoot and ideal in a bathroom environment.*

BELOW *Vinyls are available in a wide choice of patterns, so take time when choosing the most appropriate look to ensure it blends with other features and decoration in the room.*

vinyl

Vinyl is a popular choice in bathrooms because of its practical properties and the decorative nature of its finish. It can be tailored towards plain or highly patterned designs depending on personal taste. Quality varies considerably, but this means that you can have a vinyl floor covering even on a limited budget. If luxury is your aim, however, there are thick, high-quality vinyls available that are extremely comfortable underfoot.

laying a subfloor ⚡⚡

Before any floor covering is laid it is first necessary to prepare the subfloor to make it suitable for accepting the floor covering. This is of particular pertinence in bathrooms where the damp atmosphere can make greater demands on the flooring. Preparing the subfloor can broadly be divided into two categories depending on whether the existing floor is concrete or wooden.

flooring

concrete floors

Concrete is an ideal base for flooring because of its rigidity. With new screeds, the concrete must be totally dry before a new flooring can be laid. This can take up to several months, depending upon the thickness of the screed. For an old screed, the general condition of the surface will require attention. For example, you may need to fill holes or apply a self-levelling compound to establish a perfectly level surface.

tools for the job

club hammer & bolster chisel

pointing trowel

stiff-bristled brush

paintbrush

plastering trowel

power drill & mixing attachment

bucket

protective goggles

1 Use a club hammer and bolster chisel to knock off any high points on the surface of the concrete

screed. These may otherwise protrude into or even cut through the floor covering and risk damage.

2 Fill any major depressions or holes in the concrete with either a mortar mix or a stiff mix of the self-levelling compound.

3 Sweep the floor to remove any loose material and apply a coat of pva solution (1 part pva to 5 parts water) to stabilize the floor surface.

4 Mix up a quantity of the self-levelling compound in a bucket, adding water according to the manufacturer's guidelines. The mixing can be done by hand, but by far the easiest method is to use a power drill

with a mixing attachment. To avoid any splashing, make sure you both turn on and switch off the drill only when the mixing attachment is below the surface level of the compound. In any case, it is important always to wear protective goggles when mixing with a drill attachment.

5 When correctly mixed, pour the self-levelling compound immediately onto the screed surface, smoothing it across the entire floor area with a plastering trowel. As the name suggests, the compound produces a good level of its own accord as it dries, so you need not produce a perfectly level covering. Leave to dry overnight, then remove rough areas with abrasive paper.

tips of the trade

Self-levelling compound will not settle well on floors that have been treated with a bitumen base, or had a previous floor covering with a bituminous backing. In such cases, ensure all traces of bitumen have been removed from the floor surface before applying the self-levelling compound.

wooden floors

Again, the general condition of an existing wooden floor will determine its suitability for a particular floor covering. The type of wooden board will also have a bearing on the amount of preparation required. For example, a chipboard subfloor may need no further preparation if a laminate or vinyl floor is to be laid, but for hard tiles a further ply subfloor will need to be laid. Standard floorboards generally require the most preparation.

preparing floorboards

Certain procedures must be carried out prior to laying any floor covering or subfloor on floorboards. Ensure that all the boards are securely positioned. Remove the nails from any loose boards and screw them back in place to prevent creaking and movement in the future. For obvious structural and safety reasons, take care not to fix through any water, electrical or gas supply pipes below surface level.

laying hardboard

Hardboard is commonly used to level out uneven floorboards and can either be stapled or nailed in place. It is generally supplied in 120 x 60cm (4 x 2ft) sheets and should be nailed down at 10cm (4in) centres. Again, make sure the nails are long enough to fix the hardboard but will not protrude above floor level.

tools for the job

hammer
craft knife
straight edge
tape measure
pencil
scissors
jigsaw

tips of the trade

Flooring-grade hardboard is ideal for a subfloor, since it has been treated and is less likely to expand with changes in atmospheric conditions. Allow it to acclimatize in the room for at least 24 hours prior to fixing.

1 Attach the hardboard to the existing floorboards, butting the sheets together so that joins between subsequent rows of hardboard are staggered. To cut sheets down to size, score along their surface with a craft knife and straight edge, then snap off the unwanted board.

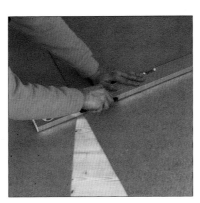

2 Use a template to cut hardboard so that it fits around awkward shapes. Cut numerous slits across a one side of a piece of paper and position it around the shape, in this case at the bottom of a basin pedestal. Mould the slits up and around the pedestal and draw a pencil line at the board/pedestal junction.

3 Cut along the pencil line and transfer this profile onto a piece of hardboard already cut to size.

4 Cut the hardboard down to size with a jigsaw. Once trimmed, fit it in place at the base of the pedestal.

laying vinyl ⚒⚒⚒⚒

Vinyl flooring comes in a variety of styles and is easily cleaned and comfortable underfoot. It is, however, relatively difficult to lay as there is very little room for error when cutting vinyl to fit. The best technique is to make a template before you begin to cut. This can be a tedious task, but is very useful for cutting the vinyl to an approximate size before final trimming is carried out.

tools for the job

scissors
straight edge or bolster chisel
craft knife
notch spreader
sealant gun or dispenser

laying the vinyl

1 Make a paper template of the floor. Allow the paper to lip up onto the wall and cut to fit around obstacles such as toilets. Tape all joins to ensure the sheets are secure. Crease the paper into the junction between floor and skirting, and draw a guideline at this point.

2 Remove the template from the floor and cut along the guideline. Tape the template on top of the vinyl, pattern-side up, and adjust its position to ensure trimming occurs in the most appropriate areas. Cut around the template allowing for an extra 5cm (2in), which will be trimmed when the vinyl is fitted. Leave the same 5cm (2in) vinyl excess around fixtures.

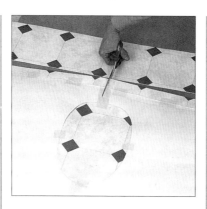

3 Remove the template and lay the vinyl out in the bathroom. Allow the excess to lip up onto the wall or skirting board surface. Crease the vinyl into the floor/skirting board junction to check that there is a consistent excess all the way around its perimeter.

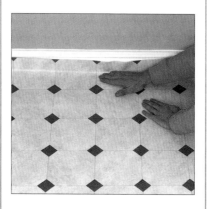

4 To ensure a precise fit, crease the vinyl into the floor/skirting junction. A long straight edge can be used for this but a bolster chisel allows more pressure to be applied on a smaller area, making the proximity to the floor junction more precise. Cut through the vinyl at the creased junction with a craft knife, moving the bolster along to the next area for trimming. Regularly change the craft knife to maintain an accurate cut.

5 A slightly different trimming method is needed to produce an accurate cut around fixtures such as toilets and basin pedestals. Allow the vinyl to lip up the obstacle in the usual way. Make small vertical cuts down the overlap to the junction it makes with the floor surface. Take care not to scratch the obstacle, in this case a toilet, with the craft knife. Care must also be taken not to overcut or to allow the vinyl to tear. Leave a gap of about 1cm (⅜in) between cuts.

6 Cut off each vinyl 'tab' made by the vertical cuts, precisely trimming along the junction between the fixture base and floor surface. Gradually work around the base until the vinyl fits perfectly.

generally a more sensible choice for joining vinyl, especially if the join will be situated in a well used part of the room. The bond made by the adhesive tends to be longer lasting than that made by tape. Apply adhesive over the join area with a notched spreader.

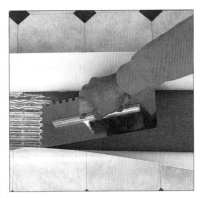

to squeeze a bead of silicone along the junction, then smooth the silicone with a wetted finger.

7 Once the entire sheet of vinyl has been accurately trimmed to fit, attention can be turned to securing it in place. Some heavier-duty vinyls may need no physical fixing to the floor surface. In a bathroom, however, it is always advisable to create some sort of seal around the edge of the vinyl, since this will help to prevent any water from penetrating beneath the vinyl surface and damaging the subfloor. Double-sided flooring tape is the ideal material for securing the vinyl in place. Simply fold the vinyl back around the room perimeter and apply the tape directly, next to the skirting board. Remove the tape backing and fold the vinyl back down to secure.

waterproofing

It is well worth adding an extra seal around the edge of the vinyl to act as a further barrier against water seepage. A bead of silicone sealant applied along the junction between the skirting board and the edge of the vinyl will form a relatively watertight barrier.

1 Apply masking tape along the skirting board and floor surface on either side of the junction, keeping as even a gap as possible between the two strips of tape.

3 Before the silicone dries, remove the tape to reveal a good watertight seal at the junction. You may need to smooth the sealant once more before leaving it to dry.

8 Where more than one sheet of vinyl has been used in a large bathroom, it may be necessary to join two lengths in part of the room. If this is the case, try to plan it so that two factory edges will make the join, as these will be more accurate than hand cut ones. Either double-sided tape or flooring adhesive may be used to secure the join. The adhesive option is

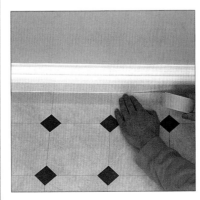

2 Cut the nozzle of a tube of silicone sealant to a diameter that spans slightly more than the gap left between the two strips of masking tape. Use a sealant gun or dispenser

👍
tips of the trade

• **Room temperature** – Vinyl becomes more pliable in warm temperatures, so it is a good idea to keep the heating on full in the bathroom while you are fitting the vinyl. This makes it easier to crease the vinyl into the wall junctions.

• **Using a hairdryer** – Accurate creasing can be very difficult, especially when dealing with thick vinyl. Employing a hairdryer to warm the vinyl along the junctions can ease the process by softening the vinyl.

• **Bath panels** – Always remove any adjacent bath panels when fitting vinyl to allow the vinyl to run underneath the panel. Before replacing the bath panel, apply a bead of silicone sealant along the junction between the panel and the vinyl to create a watertight seal.

laying hard tiles ⚒⚒⚒

Hard tiles are ideal for bathrooms because of their durability and looks. However, you need to plan work thoroughly and use the correct techniques in order to maximize both these qualities. If the tiles are unglazed, it is important to seal them with a proprietary sealing solution. Otherwise, their surface can become ingrained with adhesive and grout, which can be difficult to clean off. The majority of floor tiles are supplied with a glazed surface, which makes application more simple.

where to start

Most rooms are not totally square , so starting by laying full tiles along a skirting/wall junction is not usually an option since slight imperfections in wall alignment will become magnified as the tile design progresses across the floor. You should therefore start by finding the centre of the room. Attach a chalk line between opposing walls, pull it taut and snap the line onto the floor surface to provide a guideline. Repeat this process on the other opposing walls. The point at which the lines bisect is the centre of the room. All tiling designs should be planned from this point. Lay them dry first in order to determine the best starting point, which is ideally on a wall with few obstacles, away from the main bathroom fittings. You can then draw another guideline to show the starting line for the first full row of tiles. This line should be adjusted so that any cut tiles needed around the edge of the room are balanced.

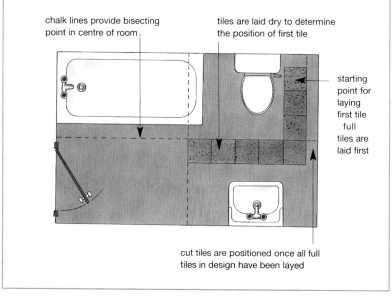

chalk lines provide bisecting point in centre of room

tiles are laid dry to determine the position of first tile

starting point for laying first tile full tiles are laid first

cut tiles are positioned once all full tiles in design have been layed

laying the tiles

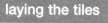

tools for the job

adjustable spanners

basin wrench

tile cutter & tile saw

1 In this example, standard tiles are being laid onto a plywood subfloor (see pages 82 3 for more information on laying subfloors). Secure wooden battens along the starting guideline and at right angles to this line to provide a good edge to butt the tiles against. Apply adhesive with a notched spreader in the area where the first tiles are to be laid.

2 Position the first tile, allowing it to bed into the adhesive before pressing it firmly in place.

3 Continue to add tiles, keeping consistent gaps between each tile using pieces of card as spacers.

4 Every now and again use a spirit level to check that all surfaces are flush. Make sure that no tile edges protrude above surface level or sink below it.

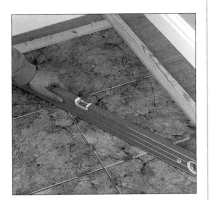

5 When all the whole tiles have been laid, fill in around the edge of the room with cut tiles. It is best to let the main body of tiles dry overnight before completing the edge, since you will have to stand on the tiles when measuring.

6 Draw guidelines on tiles that need to be cut. Use a tile cutter to score and snap along the lines.

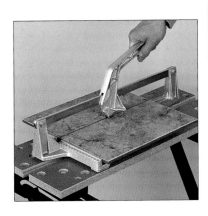

7 A tile saw is the ideal tool for cutting curves. Use the template technique shown in steps 3 and 4 on page 83 to draw the correct guideline for cutting.

8 Once all the tiles have been laid and the adhesive is dry, mix some grout and fill the joints between the tiles. Press the grout firmly in place and wipe away any excess.

Hard tiles can also be applied to the walls and boxed-in areas of a bathroom for an integrated, watertight and easy-to-clean finish. See pages 100-5 for tiling walls.

laying soft tiles ⚒⚒

Plan the layout, design, order of work and best starting point in the same way as you would for hard tiles (see diagram on page 86). However, soft tiles can be laid on plywood or hardboard – ideally flooring grade – or concrete screed as long as they are perfectly smooth and dry. In the latter case, you will probably need to lay a self-levelling compound on top of the screed in order to provide a stable surface for the tiles.

laying cork tiles

There are two types of soft tile: vinyl and cork. In this example, cork tiles are laid, but the technique employed for both types is very similar. Soft tiles can be stuck to the floor with tile adhesive, which should be applied to the floor rather than the tiles themselves, but the ones used here have a self-adhesive backing.

tools for the job

pencil & tape measure
chalk line
paintbrush
craft knife
scissors

1 Prime the subfloor to seal the surface and improve adhesion between the tiles and floor. A pva (polyvinyl adhesive) solution (5 parts water to 1 part pva) is ideal for this, or you can purchase a proprietary sealer recommended by the tile manufacturer.

2 Draw a starting guideline in the usual way (see page 86). Then peel the backing from the first tile, making sure that the adhesive does not come into contact with any other surface at this stage.

3 Carefully position the first tile, making initial contact with the edge of the tile along the pencil guideline. Repositioning can only take place before the tile is firmly pressed in place, so always take time at this stage to be sure of tile placement.

4 Lower the other edge in place and press firmly across the whole surface ensuring that it makes good contact with the subfloor.

5 Continue to add tiles, butting the edge of each new tile up against the edge of the previous one. Make sure that the joint is as tight as possible so that water will not be able to penetrate along tile edges.

6 As with any tiling, position all the full tiles before returning to the edges to fill in gaps and the areas around fittings. For awkward shapes such as basin pedestals, use a paper template to provide an accurate guide for cutting. Cut a number of slits in the piece of paper (which itself should be cut to tile size) in the area that the tile will come into contact with the obstacle. Allow the flaps of paper to overlap up the pedestal, and draw a pencil guideline at the junction between the pedestal and the floor.

7 Cut away the flaps of paper and position the template on a full tile. Draw a guideline on the tile.

8 Use sharp scissors or a craft knife to cut out the unwanted section of tile. Remove the backing paper and position the tile.

9 To deal with straight cuts around the edge of the room, take measurement requirements and transfer them to the tiles. Alternatively,

use the slightly more professional technique of placing a full tile on top of the first full tile next to the area that requires a cut tile. Put another tile on top of this one but slide it over to touch the skirting surface. Cut along the edge of the top tile and through the one below, taking care not to cut down to the one at floor level.

Instead of cutting the tile in position, as shown, with the risk of cutting the tiles below, beginners are best advised to substitute a pencil in place of a craft knife to mark the tile rather than cut it. The marked tile can then be removed, cut to size and fitted.

10 Remove the top tile and pick up the cutaway section of the one below. This should fit perfectly in the gap between the last full tile and the skirting board.

👍
tips of the trade

Vinyl tiles generally require no additional treatment once they have been laid. Cork tiles, however, usually need two or three coats of a sealant recommended by the manufacturer in order to provide the watertight surface that is essential in a bathroom.

Cork tiles provide an ideal bathroom floor surface that wears well and can withstand the constant attacks of a humid atmosphere.

wooden floorboards ⟋⟋

Wooden floorboards require a fair amount of preparation work in order to achieve an attractive and durable finish, especially if the floor is old or has previous decorative coatings applied to it. For new floorboards, preparation is much easier since coatings can be applied directly to the new wood. Much of the sequence of steps in this example relates to boards that have had previous decorative coatings that need to be stripped before new finishes can be applied.

where to start

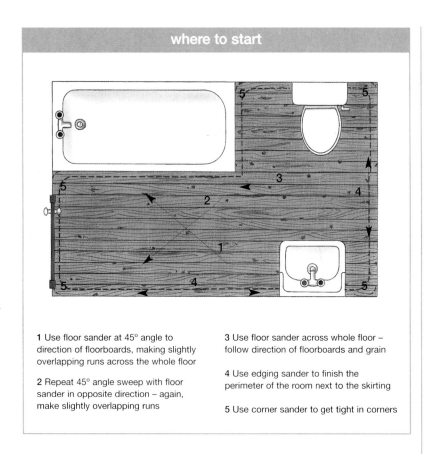

1 Use floor sander at 45° angle to direction of floorboards, making slightly overlapping runs across the whole floor

2 Repeat 45° angle sweep with floor sander in opposite direction – again, make slightly overlapping runs

3 Use floor sander across whole floor – follow direction of floorboards and grain

4 Use edging sander to finish the perimeter of the room next to the skirting

5 Use corner sander to get tight in corners

tools for the job

hammer & nail punch

drum sander

edging sander

corner sander

vacuum cleaner

cloth

paintbrush

preparing the floor

1 As the name suggests, a drum sander has a revolving drum or cylinder onto which the sandpaper is attached. Secure the sandpaper in place with a retaining bar held with screws. The frequency at which the abrasive paper needs replacing will depend on the condition of the floor of your particular bathroom. You will also achieve the best finish by reducing the coarseness or grade of sandpaper with each sweep of the floor. In this way, as the grade becomes finer, an increasingly smooth finish is achieved, essential for walking on with bare feet.

Electric sanding machines are best for wooden floorboards. These can be hired by the day from a local outlet. Three types of machine are generally required – a large drum sander copes with the central floor area, an edging sander deals with the edges and a corner sander gains access to the corners of the room. Using sanders is a messy job, so it is important to take a few precautions to make sure that dust and debris does not spread throughout the rest of your home. If possible, mask around the edge of the bathroom door to prevent dust from being transported to other areas in the house, and open the window to increase ventilation. A dust mask and goggles are essential equipment, and ear defenders are also a good idea. The illustration above demonstrates the best way to approach sanding floorboards. As with all machinery, always read the manufacturer's guidelines before use.

👍

tips of the trade

Make sure that all loose boards are secured in place before beginning to sand and also that any nail heads are punched in below the floor surface. Failure to do this could damage sanders and/or tear sandpaper, either of which will lead to greater expense.

2 Beginning with the drum sander, sand the floor at a 45° angle to the floorboards, as shown in the illustration opposite. Always tilt back the sander before starting it up, then carefully lower the drum onto the floor surface. Starting the sander when it is flat on the floor can cause it to produce unsightly scars or gouges in the wood. Continue the sequence with the drum sander as shown in the diagram.

3 Once the central area of the floor is complete, use an edging sander around the perimeter of the room and obstacles such as toilet pans and basin pedestals. The edging sander is also useful for finishing central areas of the floor that may be particularly ingrained. Sometimes the design of the drum sander does not allow the roller to be effective in small depressions in the floor surface, which makes the edging sander, with its orbital action, much more useful in this case. It is worth taking time at this stage to get the best finish possible.

4 The pointed end of the hand-held corner sander is ideal for getting right into the corners of the room that are impossible to access with either the drum or edging sander.

finishing the floor

Once all previous coatings of stain, varnish or paint have been removed from the floorboards, you can apply the new finishing coats that will provide an attractive and watertight finish. In this case, a simple varnish has been applied.

1 Brush the floor to remove as much dust as possible, then use a vacuum cleaner to suck up any further debris. Pay particular attention to joints between floorboards and along the skirting.

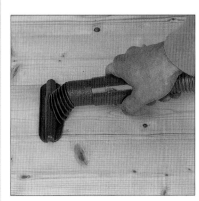

2 Use a cloth dampened in white spirit to clean the floor surface thoroughly and remove any remaining fine dust particles.

3 Apply varnish to the floor allowing the bristles of the paintbrush to follow the direction of the wood grain.

4 Add two or three coats of varnish, sanding with fine abrasive paper between coats.

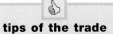

tips of the trade

Wooden floorboards need several coats of stain, paint or varnish. Try to use acrylic quick-drying varieties so that several coats can be applied in one day.

laying a laminate floor ///

Laminate floors are a smoother version of floorboards. There are many different types available including ones that are suitable for bathroom use. Always check the manufacturer's guidelines to make sure that your choice is appropriate for the bathroom, because there is often nothing obviously visible about the design of a laminate floor to indicate its suitability. It is the method of manufacture that dictates whether it can to cope with the moist atmosphere of a bathroom.

where to start

Laminate floors are supplied as boards of various sizes depending on the manufacturer. They are often 90cm (3ft) in length but may be much longer. Whatever the length, rows are built up in turn as you gradually progress across the floor surface. The joints between subsequent rows are also staggered to form a brick bond pattern that adds strength as well as improving the look of the floor. Cutting and trimming laminate flooring can be tricky, so it is best to start with the longest extent in the room that is free from obstacles. Ideally, this will be the longest wall in the bathroom with the fewest fittings. Although walls are not always perfectly true or square, slight imperfections are not as noticeable with laminate flooring as they would be with the more geometrically accurate designs of a tiled floor. It is, therefore, perfectly acceptable to use a skirting board or wall/floor junction as a starting point. However, if there are major undulations in a wall surface, you may need to offset your starting line slightly to achieve a more balanced effect.

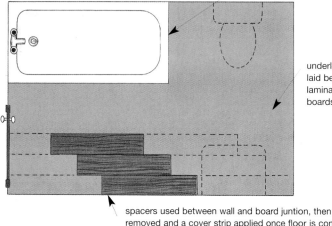

tile cuts below fittings

underlay laid before laminate boards

spacers used between wall and board juntion, then removed and a cover strip applied once floor is complete

👍 tips of the trade

Before laying a laminate floor, consider removing the skirting first. You can then lay the floor more easily and reposition the skirting after the floor is complete to give a neat edge.

👍 tips of the trade

If possible, lay laminate floors before obstacles such as basin pedestals are installed. Also consider having a wall-mounted basin in the bathroom to minimize problems of floor fitting.

tools for the job

tape measure
pencil
craft knife or scissors
panel saw or jigsaw
hammer
knocking block
jemmy
sponge
mitresaw

laying the floor

1 Roll out underlay on top of your subfloor, butting adjoining lengths as you progress across the floor surface. Underlay is very lightweight and is supplied in rolls, which make it easy to apply. Thickness will depend on the manufacturer.

2 Fit the underlay up to the edges of the skirting boards but do not overlap the skirting or wall surface. Where necessary, cut the underlay using a craft knife or sharp pair of scissors.

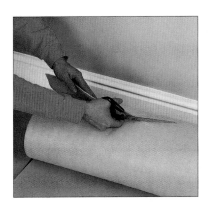

3 Position the first length of laminate flooring against the skirting board at your chosen starting position. The groove side of the board should face the skirting with the tongue side pointing into the middle of the room. Position spacing blocks between the edge of the board and the skirting to maintain a consistent gap.

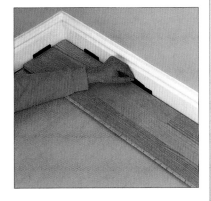

4 On the second row of boards, cut the first length so that you can create a brick bond pattern of jointing, with the joints of each row staggered. Cut the boards with either a panel saw or jigsaw.

5 Apply wood glue or an adhesive recommended by the floor manufacturer along the tongue of the first row of boards.

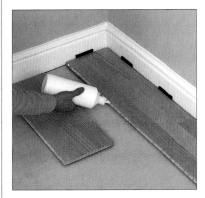

6 Position the cut length, with its groove aligned with the tongue of the first row of boards. Use a hammer and knocking block to tap it into position. Never use a hammer directly on the tongue of a board because it will damage it.

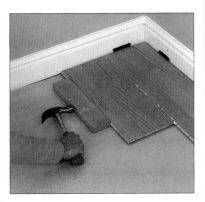

7 Wipe excess adhesive from the floor surface before it has a chance to dry. It can be difficult to clean off later.

8 Keep adding boards building up the rows across the floor. When you reach the end of a row, use a jemmy to knock the interlocking mechanism of the tongue and groove at the ends of boards into place.

9 When the floor is complete, remove the spacing blocks and add a quadrant moulding around the edge. In this case, the manufacturer has supplied a matching strip with a self-adhesive tape to fix it to the skirting junction. You will need to mitre the ends of each moulding so that they fit neatly into the corners of the room.

TYPES OF SUBFLOOR

Laminate floors are extremely versatile. They can be laid onto concrete as long as it is totally dry. The manufacturer may also stipulate the use of a plastic membrane before laying the floor. Otherwise, laminate floors can be laid over chipboard, hardboard or plywood subfloors.

laying mosaic tiles

Some manufacturers now produce mosaic tiles suitable for floor use. They are supplied in sheets, which allows a large number to be laid at any one time – single tile application would be a very labour-intensive and time-consuming project, even for the smallest of bathrooms. When laying mosaic tiles, your first concern must be to make sure that they are laid as evenly and flat as possible so that they are comfortable underfoot.

flooring

94

tips of the trade

If the edges of mosaic tiles lift above floor level, their small size means that they will be uncomfortable underfoot, so it is vital that the surface onto which they are laid is level. Concrete or plywood subfloors are ideal as other types rarely provide enough rigidity. Make sure there are no protruding nails or bumps in the floor's surface.

tools for the job

tape measure & pencil

hammer

notched spreader

mini roller

grout spreader

scissors

tile nibblers

sponge

1 Choosing a suitable starting point when tiling with mosaics is vital and varies slightly from the approach taken when laying larger floor tiles. However, as with larger tiles, it is important to start laying the mosaics from one wall in the room, using a batten to act as an initial supporting barrier to butt the tiles up against. Position the batten close to the wall, ideally about two or three tile widths away from the skirting board. (When the batten is removed it will be easy to fill the remaining gap with the small tiles.)

Tile sheets are not applied directly next to the skirting because, if the room is not totally square, even a

small angle of difference will become exaggerated in the finished tile design. The second batten shown here (fixed at 90° to the first) provides a good guideline for producing a square design that will appear balanced and in alignment with the walls of the room, even if they are not totally square. Spread adhesive onto the subfloor in the area where the first mosaic sheets are to be positioned.

2 Remove the backing from the first sheet of mosaic tiles. This backing may be made of plastic or paper and its only function is to make the sheets easier to handle before being laid in place.

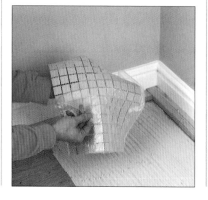

3 Position the sheet of mosaic tiles, adhesive side down, so that the edges of the tiles on two sides of the sheet rest against the right angle formed by the battens. A mosaic sheet is not rigid like a standard floor tile, so pay particular attention that each tile edge is in the correct place and that none is skewed out of position. Fix any that are misaligned before the adhesive has a chance to dry.

4 Run a mini roller over the surface of the sheet. Apply even pressure across its expanse to bed the mosaic tiles into the adhesive and ensure that each tile is as flat as possible.

5 Lay the next sheet of tiles in the same way, inserting pieces of cardboard as spacers between each sheet to maintain a consistent gap between them.

6 As mentioned before, the flexible nature of a mosaic sheet can allow single tiles to move slightly out of position. Rather than checking and repositioning individual tiles one at a time, use a grout spreader to maintain consistent and straight gaps between rows of tiles. Where tiles appear out of position, simply press the blade of the spreader into the gaps between them to straighten any tile edges that are not aligned.

7 Once the central floor area is complete, apply tiles around the edge of the room. It is best to leave the full mosaic sheets to dry overnight before tackling the edges in case you dislodge them from position. Remove the battens, then cut tile sheets to the desired size to fit in the gap between the full sheets and skirting board edge.

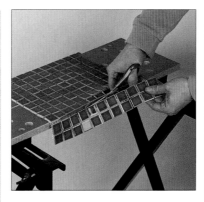

8 Apply adhesive along the gap in the usual way and carefully position the strips of tiles. Again, use a mini roller to make sure that they are bedded in sufficiently and level with the surrounding tiles. Check that they are aligned correctly with the tiles that have already been laid.

9 You may need to use single tiles cut to size to follow the curved profile of obstacles such as a basin pedestal or the base of a toilet pan. Single tiles are too small to be cut with a tile cutter, so use tile nibblers to trim the unwanted portion of the tile before putting it in position.

10 Grout the floor with a grout spreader, by pushing the grout firmly into all the joints and making sure that they are all evenly filled. Try to keep the level of the grout flush with the mosaic tiles rather than raised above them. This will provide a smoother feel underfoot. Wipe away excess grout from the tiled surfaces using a damp sponge, then allow to dry overnight.

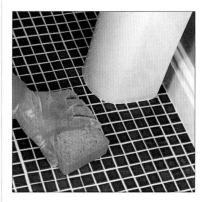

COLOURED GROUT

Try finishing mosaic tiles with coloured grout for a different finish. The colour itself is normally supplied as a powder and mixed with white grout to achieve the required intensity. Matching the wall colour can create a good effect.

ALL-OVER MOSAIC

For an all-over effect, use the same type of tiles on the walls as those used on the floor.

MOSAIC BORDER

Mosaic tiles may be used selectively on floors rather than as an overall design. For example, using large tiles in the centre of the floor with mosaic tiles around the edge can be extremely effective.

CHANGING PATTERNS

Although mosaics are supplied in sheet form, patterns can be created by using a selection of different coloured sheets or cutting single tiles from sheets and replacing them with another colour.

finishing touches

The final look of a bathroom can be enhanced
by close attention to decorative details and
those finishing touches that can make the
difference between a competent finish and one
of outstanding impact. Painting, papering and
tiling techniques are all important in producing
the finished look. Equally, small accessories
will not only enable the bathroom to funtion
efficiently, but also contribute considerably
towards an attractive finished product. Having
carried out the bulk of the hard work in actually
fitting a new bathroom, you should still take
time to complete the job properly and not
overlook the final, small details. This chapter
demonstrates how to achieve an impressive
standard of decoration and, in addition,
considers areas such as window dressings
and fitting small accessories.

Small details, such as the free-standing
soap dish and the moveable shaving
stand, transform function into style.

options for finishing

Bathroom decorations need to be durable to withstand the rigours of a damp atmosphere. Tiles are always popular because of their durable finish, and there is an astonishing array of patterns, colours and designs available. Other finishing options have been developed to cope with the demands of a bathroom and paper, paint and window dressings can now be chosen from materials that are either specific to bathroom use or made to withstand humidity.

full tile

A full-tile approach – that is, tiling all the walls from floor to ceiling – is probably the most durable choice for a bathroom. Water and condensation cannot penetrate tile surfaces, and the only area that can be damaged is the grout and sealing joints around the edges of the tiles. The extent of degradation here will often depend on how well ventilated the room is and how frequently surfaces are wiped and cleaned. Always remember that tiling an entire bathroom will take a considerable amount of time and involve a large number of cut tiles. This type of wall finish is, therefore, probably not a task for beginners and is more suited to experienced tilers. Pay particular attention to planning your work because, once you have begun tiling, it will be hard to rectify mistakes at a later date.

RIGHT *The clean, bright and polished look of tiles always provides a good finish to any bathroom layout. Different sizes and patterns can be used to break up solid areas of colour and add greater interest to the design.*

half tile

Another popular finish is to extend tiles halfway up the wall around the entire bathroom. After all, it is the lower wall area that is in closest proximity to fittings and therefore the place where most water damage will occur. The tiles in a half-tiled bathroom should also extend above the basin area and around the bathtub so you will not need to provide separate tiled splashbacks. This type of tiling job is much less daunting than a fully-tiled bathroom, particularly for beginners. Again, it is a good idea to experiment with patterns and designs when planning the layout to ensure that you achieve the most attractive result and all cut tiles are positioned as unobtrusively as possible.

LEFT *The neat lines of a half-tile finish create an elegant and well-planned look. Decorative border tiles can be used to define the edges of the design or, as in this case, a stencilled border has been applied to highlight the change between surfaces.*

paint

Bathroom paint that contains vinyl is usually the most durable choice. This is easily cleaned and unlikely to degrade as quickly as other paints. Choosing the right colour is very important because the painted surfaces in a bathroom tend to act as a frame for the bathroom suite.

wallpaper

Wallpaper is not usually the first choice of decorative finish for a bathroom because there can be problems with peeling and lifting seams. However, as long as the paper chosen is designed for bathroom use and applied carefully, it will provide a long-lasting finish. Wallpaper also adds texture to wall finishes, thereby lending the room greater depth and making the walls appear less two-dimensional.

ABOVE RIGHT *The yellow painted walls in this bathroom maximize the natural light and combine with other elements to create a fun, bright room that appeals to children.*

BELOW RIGHT *This traditional bathroom layout benefits from the choice of deep red wallpaper, which gives the room a very sumptuous and comfortable atmosphere.*

BELOW *Venetian or slatted blinds can be adjusted to let in the desired amount of light, while still retaining a degree of privacy.*

window dressing

Choosing window dressings for bathrooms can be difficult. It is usually best to avoid anything too voluminous because it can take up too much valuable space. Also, large folds of material can retain the damp and become soiled so that their finish tarnishes relatively quickly. Hence, simple blinds are popular in bathrooms because they take up less space than curtains and provide flexible degrees of privacy depending on how far they are lowered or drawn.

tiling walls – 1 ⚒

Successful bathroom tiling requires a sound knowledge of basic tiling technique. You need to adopt a methodical approach, make sure that all measurements are accurate and ensure that the vertical and horizontal lines of the design are maintained at all times. The number of obstacles found in a bathroom make this a difficult project for beginners but, as long as the basic principles are adhered to, tiling a bathroom is within the capability of most home improvement enthusiasts.

planning

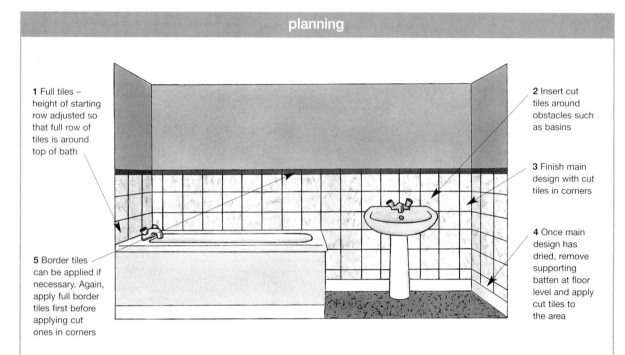

1 Full tiles – height of starting row adjusted so that full row of tiles is around top of bath

5 Border tiles can be applied if necessary. Again, apply full border tiles first before applying cut ones in corners

2 Insert cut tiles around obstacles such as basins

3 Finish main design with cut tiles in corners

4 Once main design has dried, remove supporting batten at floor level and apply cut tiles to the area

You must always plan carefully before embarking on a tiling project in the bathroom. You should take even more care than usual when deciding on the best starting point and the order of work, because a bathroom inevitably has complex areas where you will need to cut a number of tiles in various shapes. The diagram above shows a typical bathroom layout and identifies the best way of breaking down a design into different areas on the wall surface. These should be tackled in the order indicated to achieve a professional-looking finish.

You should always begin at the bottom of the wall and work upwards so that each subsequent row of tiles is supported by the previous row. Using a skirting board as the starting point is often dangerous because it may not be level. It is, therefore, much better to fix a wooden batten to the wall to support the first row of tiles using a spirit level to make sure the batten is perfectly horizontal. A tile gauge is the ideal tool for planning designs so that they are central in relation to fittings (if necessary) and for choosing the most appropriate starting points.

making a tile gauge

To create a home-made tile gauge, first cut a piece of 5cm x 2.5cm (2 x 1in) batten, which is about the length of four or five tiles. Line up tiles along the edge of the batten, positioning spacers between them to provide a consistent joint gap. Use a pencil to mark the position of the tile joints on the batten – take care to do this accurately as it will serve as a measuring tool. You can then hold the batten vertically and horizontally against the wall to work out where tile cuts will be required, and hence the best starting point to avoid any unnecessary tile cuts. Try to plan so that small slithers of tile will not be required because these are difficult to cut and can be unsightly.

tools for the job

cordless drill/driver

notched spreader

spirit level

scraper

1 Fix a piece of batten to the wall at the required starting point, using a spirit level to check that it is perfectly horizontal. Screw or nail the batten in place using the appropriate fixings. If you wish, attach a vertical batten at the starting position.

2 Use a notched spreader to apply adhesive along the bottom of the area to be tiled. Go over the area with the spreader two or three times to ensure even adhesive coverage.

3 Press the first tile firmly into place in the right-angled corner made by the two supporting battens.

4 Position the next tile and add a spacer at the top and bottom of the joint. The spacer at the top will remain in position and be covered with grout. The spacer at the bottom should be inserted at right angles to the joint, resting on the supporting batten, and is removed when the adhesive has dried.

5 Continue to build up the design in rows. Regularly hold a spirit level across the top of the tiles to check that none is out of place. When finished, remove the battens and apply cut tiles into the space if required (see pages 102–3).

6 On undulating walls, tiles may sometimes sink below the surrounding surface level or sit proud of the tile surface. In such cases, remove the tile with a scraper before the adhesive dries.

7 Adjust the level of adhesive accordingly, before repositioning the tile. In this case, the tile required extra adhesive to build it up to the surrounding tile level.

tips of the trade

• **Shuffling** – When using single-coloured tiles for all or a major part of a design, open up the boxes of tiles before you start and shuffle them to make sure that any slight differences in colour between batches are diluted across the whole design.

• **Keeping tile surface clean** – Use a damp sponge to remove excess adhesive from tile surfaces as you progress. Although adhesive can be removed when it is dry, it is much easier to wipe it away now rather than chip it off later when it has hardened.

tiling walls – 2

Most tile designs are composed of full tiles, but it is inevitable that some cutting and trimming will be required in order to finish off the edges and deal with any obstacles. A good tile cutter will help you complete this process successfully and can make the difference between sharp, accurate cuts and ones that either deviate from the desired cutting line or cause the tile to break or shatter rather than snap accurately along a scored line.

tools for the job

tape measure

pencil or felt-tip pen

hand-held or electrically operated tile-cutting machine

protective goggles

tile saw

tile nibblers

grout spreader

sponge

sealant gun or dispenser

cutting tiles by hand

Cutting requirements can be measured by either holding a full tile in position and marking the required cuts with a pencil or felt-tip pen, or measuring the space to be tiled and transferring this to a tile.

1 Position the marked tile in the machine under the cutting wheel. Push the wheel across the surface of the tile, applying slight downward pressure to score a line through the glazed surface.

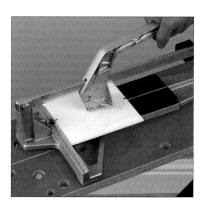

2 The second section of the tile-cutting machine is then put to use. Allow the wheel to pass off the end of the tile before applying downward pressure once again. This time the metal extensions on the machine handle press down on either side of the scored line causing the tile to snap accurately at this point.

cutting curves

It is not possible to use a tile-cutting machine to cut curves, you will need a tile saw for this purpose instead. Mark the required guideline on the tile, then saw through it. Using a tile saw is a slow process, so be prepared to take a little extra time.

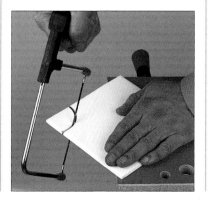

cutting out sections

You may need to use both a tile saw and some tile nibblers to remove sections from one edge of a tile. Use the saw to make the required cuts into the main body of the tile, then use nibblers to snap off the unwanted section.

electric tile-cutting machines

These can perform more functions than simple hand-held tile cutters. They are generally used when tiling floors because their robust structure is better for dealing with thicker, larger tiles. However, the price of tile-cutting machines has reduced considerably in recent years and, because they can speed up tiling, many people are buying such machines to use for all types of tiling. Operating procedures vary from machine to machine, so always read the manufacturer's guidelines carefully before use. Some protective equipment will be required, such as goggles for eye protection.

straight cuts

Most machines have a reservoir that must be filled with water. This cools the cutting wheel, which can generate considerable heat due to friction. Mark the position of cuts on the tile in the usual way, then feed the tile into the cutting wheel.

mitred cuts

It is not possible to remove slithers from a tile edge or create a mitred cut for an external corner using a hand-held cutter or a machine. However, some tile cutters have an angled stage that allows you to produce a mitred cut for internal corners.

grouting

Once all the tiles have been fixed to the wall, you need to fill all the joints with grout so that a waterproof surface is produced. The adhesive must be dry before applying grout (normally left overnight is sufficient).

1 Mix sufficient grout for the tiled area, but be aware that a small amount of grout goes a long way. Use a grout spreader to press the grout firmly into the joints between the tiles. It is important that grout fills each joint, so sweep the blade of the spreader in all directions across the tile surface in order to achieve this.

2 Remove excess grout from the tiled surface using a damp sponge. Rinse the sponge frequently to keep it free from grout build-up. Run a grout shaper or grouting tool along the joints of the grout to neaten the finish.

sealing

After tiling is complete, the joints between tiles and fittings or other surfaces must be sealed in order to provide a watertight finish. The best material for this is silicone sealant. This comes in tubes that must be loaded into a specially designed sealant gun or dispenser.

1 Apply masking tape along each side of the joint, keeping the distance between the edges of the tape as consistent as possible.

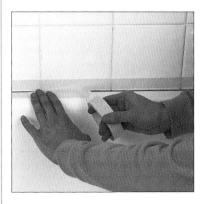

2 Expel sealant along the joint so that the edges of the sealant encroach slightly onto the masking tape. Smooth it with a wet finger.

3 Remove the masking tape while the sealant is still wet to reveal a smooth joint. If the edges of the sealant lift slightly as you remove the tape, gently smooth them again with a wet finger. Allow the sealant to dry completely (usually 24 hours).

tiling a splashback ⁄⁄⁄

In many bathrooms the splashback area behind the basin is incorporated into an entire wall of tiles. However, if this is not the case you will need to plan a separate tiled splashback. The key to achieving a good result is to make sure that the splashback is centrally positioned in relation to the basin. You can then centre the first tile on this central point and tile outwards from there, or use the centre point as a joint between the first two tiles, again working outwards.

tools for the job

tape measure & pencil
mini level
notched spreader
electric tile-cutting machine
grout spreader (optional)
protective gloves
sponge
sealant gun or dispenser

1 Measure the back edge of the basin and mark the centre point.

2 Draw a pencil guideline upwards from this point. Use a mini level to make sure that the line is vertical.

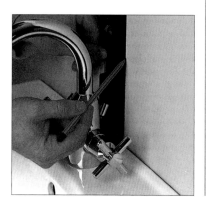

3 Mark the middle of the first tile along its top edge. This mark is only required for positioning purposes so it can be wiped off later. Apply some adhesive to the back of the tile using a small notched spreader.

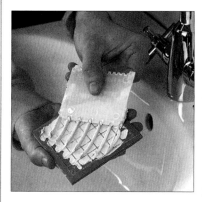

4 Position the tile by making sure that the pencil mark corresponds exactly with the vertical pencil guideline on the wall.

5 Continue to apply tiles to the wall, using spacers in joints to maintain a consistent gap between tiles. The back edge of many basins is curved. This makes tiling slightly more difficult because you will need to place card beneath the edge of the first row of tiles to maintain the correct level for the tiles. The amount of card used at a particular point depends on how much is required to keep the row level. Likewise, when border tiles are added, card will need to be used under the first ones on either side of the design in order to maintain the correct height.

6 It is usually necessary to cut border tiles at the corner of the splashback. A good effect is achieved by making mitred joints. For relief border tiles, as shown here, it is best to use an electrically operated tile-cutting machine. Again, wear protective goggles and follow the manufacturer's instructions.

7 Once the first mitred tile has been positioned, measure the next tile by holding it in place and marking the points at which the tile needs to be cut.

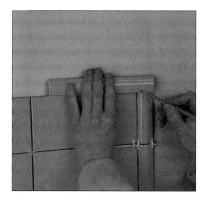

8 Position the tile, judging a joint between the mitre that is equal to the gaps between the tiles in the main part of the design.

9 Once the design is complete, allow to dry, then grout. It can be easier to use your fingers rather than a spreader to push the grout into place on tiles with a raised surface, but always wear protective gloves.

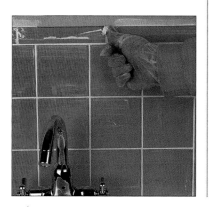

10 When you have finished grouting, apply a silicone sealant strip along the back edge of the basin. Use the technique described on page 103.

Use the technique described on page 103.

tips of the trade

• **Full tiles** – Ideally, you should only use full tiles in a splashback design because there is no way of hiding from view cut tiles that can mar the overall look of the basin. It does not usually matter if tiles overhang the edge of the basin slightly and, in many cases, a row of border tiles can provide an attractive frame.

• **Spacers** – When using spacers in conjunction with relief border tiles, it is not possible to insert them into joints flat against the wall. Instead, insert them at right angles to the wall surface and remove them once the adhesive has dried.

A tiled splashback provides a practical and decorative feature that highlights and complements a basin design.

decorative finishing ⚒

Aside from tiles, there are two other options for finishing bathroom walls: paint and wallpaper. In many instances, these finishes can be combined to good effect. It has already been emphasized that materials must be chosen carefully in order to deal with the special requirements of the bathroom environment, and below and opposite are some ideas and guidelines that relate more closely to the specifics of this problem.

paint

The primary concern when choosing paint for the bathroom is to make sure that it is washable. For this reason if you are applying emulsion it is best to choose one that contains vinyl for this reason. Eggshell is a good choice in bathrooms because it is more durable than emulsion and is equally effective on both walls and woodwork. Many people opt for gloss on woodwork because it provides the most durable finish. If you do so, consider using water-based or acrylic options as these are much more user friendly than their oil-based counterparts. They are also quick drying, so it is possible to apply more than one coat in a day. In all cases, it does no harm to apply an extra coat of paint to all surfaces to make them more long lasting. This is especially important for varnished or painted floor surfaces.

👍 tips of the trade

• **Painting equipment** – Equipment and techniques involved in painting do not change simply because you are in a bathroom environment. Always choose good-quality tools for the job, since they are much easier to use and produce the best finish. You should also make use of time-saving equipment such as rollers or paint pads, which cover surfaces quickly and efficiently. Make sure you have a few different sizes of paintbrush available, because these will come in handy when cutting in around all the various fittings.

masking up

1 When painting a bathroom, a little extra effort at the preparation stage can save a great deal of time later on. You should always cover the floor with dust sheets and keep paint overspray off fittings and fixtures by covering them. Plastic dust sheets are ideal for covering fittings such as basins and toilets. Use masking tape to hold the sheets securely in place.

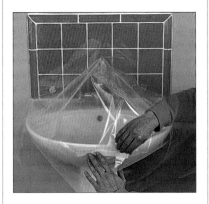

2 Masking around the edge of tiles helps to provide a neater dividing line between the wall and tiled surface. It takes some time to do but is well worth the effort.

paint improvements

1 Further improvement in the overall bathroom finish can be achieved by attention to detail and using the correct techniques throughout the decoration process. Here are just two examples of how you can refine the finish of your bathroom. First, you can paint any pipes that are not boxed in to blend with wall colour, thereby making them less obvious to the naked eye.

2 You can also paint bath panels. It is best to do this when they are in a horizontal position because paint runs can be a problem unless you are particularly vigilant.

wallpaper

There are two schools of thought on wallpaper in bathrooms. One maintains that vinyl papers are ideal, while the other expounds exactly the opposite theory. Many people consider vinyl papers an attractive option because they are easily cleaned. However, their shiny surface allows water to run directly off it, which means that any condensation in the room becomes accentuated on this type of finish.

Some people, therefore, choose standard papers that can still be cleaned but do not show up condensation so easily. The problem here is that they are generally not as durable as vinyl papers. Each variety has its advantages and disadvantages, although in both cases the problems can be dispelled to a large extent if ventilation systems in the room are adequate.

stripping old coverings

Previously papered walls must be stripped before redecoration. Wallpaper can rarely be papered or painted over with any degree of success in any room in the home. In a bathroom, where condensation damage is likely to be at its greatest, it is almost certain that decorating over the top of existing paper will produce a less than adequate finish. Therefore, it is always best to remove old wall coverings before redecorating the bathroom.

👍

tips of the trade

If you are renovating the entire bathroom, strip the walls when the old suite has been removed but before the new one is installed. In this way, all the messy work is carried out prior to any new installation and the new fittings will not get covered in dust.

1 Remove as much paper as possible from the wall surface while it is dry. This is easy to do if you pull the paper away at lifting seams. The top layer of wallpaper often comes away quite easily leaving just the backing paper on the wall surface.

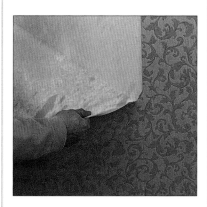

2 Cover the backing paper with hot water and allow it to soak in for a few minutes before scraping the paper from the wall.

USING A STEAM STRIPPER

For walls that have a number of layers of paper, or where there is a lot of stripping to do, you may be able to save time by using a steam stripper. These can be hired relatively cheaply on a day-rate basis. That said, the price of steam strippers has become more competitive in recent years and, if you have a lot of stripping to do, you may find it more economical to buy one outright. Be sure to read the manufacturer's guidelines for use.

protecting wallpaper

1 Several measures can be taken to protect wallpaper, such as applying a coat of matt varnish or emulsion glaze. Always conduct a test patch first because this type of coating is not suitable for all papers.

2 Allow the edge of the paper to extend slightly into any areas to be tiled. The tiles will prevent the paper from lifting at a later date.

3 Apply silicone sealant at the junction between wallpaper and skirting to help hold the paper down.

fitting blinds ⚲

Although curtains can be used in bathrooms, blinds are usually more suitable. They take up less room than curtains and can be opened or closed to varying degrees, so that adequate light can enter the room while still providing the required privacy. Choose blind material carefully because not all fabric is suited to the humid atmosphere of the bathroom. It is also important to choose a fabric that is easily cleaned and durable.

types of blind

The mechanism by which blinds are raised and lowered varies but most are controlled by cords. In many cases there is more than one cord, because the blind has a number of different settings in order to let in varying amounts of light and provide different degrees of privacy. Also, not all blinds are raised or lowered in the same way as those shown here. Manufacturers are constantly designing new mechanisms to produce extra interest and increase ease of function. Four of the most common types of blind design are shown here.

roller blinds

As their name suggests, these blinds operate on a roller system. When raised, the blind material wraps around the roller. A pull cord is used to close the blind, unrolling the material in front of the window. In a recessed window, roller blinds can be fitted outside or inside the recess. The latter option takes up less space

and provides a more 'fitted' look, although measurements must be as accurate as possible so that the blind does not touch the walls on either side of the recess when it is raised or lowered. Designs vary between manufacturers, but most are installed by fixing the head rail into specially designed brackets attached to the window frame.

roman blinds

Roman blinds are slightly more complex in design than roller blinds, because there is a system of horizontal battens sewn into the blind material. When the blind is raised, these battens gather the material into a number of equal-sized folds.

venetian blinds

Venetian blinds – sometimes called slatted blinds – are made from a number of strips of wood or aluminium that are connected by cords to hold them in position. Their design allows the blind to be fully opened or closed like solid blinds, but there is also a function that tilts

the single slats of the blind to adjust light levels and intensity. They are, therefore, ideal for creating a sense of privacy in the bathroom without having to lose too much natural light.

vertical blinds

Vertical blinds are closely related to venetian blinds, in that they are made from slatted sections that can be adjusted to admit different levels of light into the room. However, when totally opened or closed they behave more like curtains because their vertical design means that the blind sections are drawn across the width of the main window surface.

fitting a venetian blind

In a recessed window, venetian blinds can be fitted outside or inside the recess. If fitted inside, measurements must be accurate so that the blind does not touch the walls during use.

tools for the job

screwdriver

bradawl

cordless drill/driver

1 The retaining brackets for the head rail are usually designed with a hinged section that should be opened before fixing them to the window frame. You can usually do this by hand but you can use a screwdriver as a lever to open up the bracket if it is stiff.

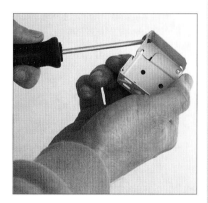

tips of the trade

When fitting any type of blind inside a recess, measurements must be accurate. If the blind is too wide, it will simply not fit because there is no flexibility in head rails or rollers. Always double-check measurements, taking care to measure the width of the recess at the top, middle and lower levels. In many cases, a window recess may vary slightly in size across its dimensions. Thus in order for a blind to fit, the narrowest point must be used when calculating the width of blind to buy.

2 Hold the bracket in place at the top corner of the window frame. Use a bradawl to mark through the screw holes and into the frame below. Remove the bracket from its position and use a cordless drill/driver to make pilot holes for the screws at the marked points.

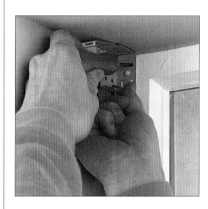

3 Reposition the bracket and screw it firmly in place. Repeat steps 1–3 for the corresponding bracket at the other corner.

4 Insert the venetian blind into the brackets, allowing each end of the head rail to slot into place.

5 Once in position, snap the hinged sections of the brackets closed, thereby locking the head rail in place.

6 Most venetian blinds are supplied with a pelmet. This is generally attached to the head rail using self-adhesive Velcro pads. Attach the pads along the inside of the pelmet and their corresponding sections along the head rail, taking care to marry them up.

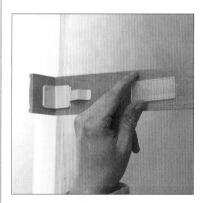

7 Align the Velcro pads and press the pelmet firmly in position on the head rail.

fitting accessories ⤴

All the small accessories in a bathroom, such as soap dishes, toothbrush holders and non-heated towel rails, supply additional storage areas that make the best use of space. They also provide the finishing touches to the overall look of the bathroom, which will make your decorative scheme look complete and the room welcoming. Many of these accessories are available as sets so that you can achieve a coordinated finish.

The fitting mechanisms on accessories vary but it is usually the case that specially designed brackets are attached to the wall surface first, then the actual fitting is attached to the bracket and held in place with a discreetly positioned grub screw. This two-part fitting process can be difficult because you need to make sure that brackets align correctly with fittings. Alternatively, the actual fixing bracket is integral to the fitting and, once in place, a cover or cap is fitted over the bracket to provide an attractive finish.

Installing accessories on tiled surfaces requires a specific technique to make the appropriate pilot holes for wall plug and screw fixings.

fixing into tiles

Fixing accessories to plaster walls, whether solid or hollow, can be achieved using the correct wall plugs and screws, and the same is true for tiled surfaces. However, you need to use a specially designed drill bit that is strong enough to penetrate a tile accurately. Accuracy is the key point here because a hole drilled in the wrong place cannot simply be filled and repainted in the way that you would with plaster walls. Also, even though tiles have a very strong surface, they can shatter or crack

if the wrong technique is used. A standard masonry drill bit may well go through some tiles, but it is often the case that while piercing the tiled surface, the coarseness of the bit can break away glazed sections of tile around the hole.

tools for the job

felt-tip pen

tape measure

cordless drill/driver

screwdriver

1 Take your time when deciding on the precise position for the fitting – in this case a towel ring – because mistakes are not easy to rectify on a tiled surface. The bracket for the accessory should be fixed in as central a position on the tile as possible. The closer you move towards the edge of a tile, the more likely that drill vibrations will cause it to crack. Hold the fitting in place with one hand and use a felt-tip pen to mark through the screw holes onto the tile surface below.

2 Remove the fitting from the tile surface and cover the marked points with masking tape. It should still be possible to see the marks through the tape, but if they are not obvious renew them on top of the tape. The reason that masking tape is applied over the drilling points is that the shiny surface of the tile can cause the drill bit to slip, which makes accurate drilling impossible and can lead to scratching. The masking tape adds some grip and keeps the point of the bit in place.

3 Insert the tile drill bit into the drill, making sure it is securely held in place. A tile drill bit looks like a miniature javelin or spear.

4 Holding the drill bit against the marked point on the tile, start up on the drill a low speed. This will create a tiny indentation in the tile surface that will allow the bit to gain a good grip before the speed is increased. Once this initial break is made, use the drill in the normal way to penetrate through the tile surface and into the wall below. Holding a vacuum cleaner nozzle below the hole while you drill will improve the aesthetic finish of the tiled surface, because it prevents the dust produced when drilling through tiles from falling down and resting in grout joints or sealant beads at the base of the wall. Even if this dust is wiped off, there is often unsightly staining of the grout or sealant. By using the vacuum to remove dust as you drill, there is no need to clean up afterwards and the grout or sealant cannot become stained.

5 Once the holes are drilled, remove the masking tape from the tile surface. Insert wall plugs into the holes. These are usually supplied with the fitting – if not, choose some suitable ones from your supply or buy some if you do not have any already. The plugs will generally slip into the holes, easily tightening as the head of the plug becomes flush with the wall surface. In some cases, you may need to use the butt end of a hammer to knock the plug into position. Be sure to use only the butt end of the hammer, because using the other end will risk breaking the tile.

6 Reposition the fitting and screw it in place. It is always best to use a hand-held screwdriver for this because it offers greater control regarding the amount of pressure exerted. If a cordless screwdriver is used, there can be a danger of over-tightening, which could crack the tiled surface so that the tile will need to be replaced.

7 Finally, screw the covering cap in place to obscure the fixing mechanism. This may attach with a grub screw or simply be a threaded fitting that is screwed into place by hand.

INSTALLING TWO OR MORE BRACKETS INTO TILES

In the example shown here, only one bracket is required to hold the fitting in place. However, for larger fittings such as horizontal towel rails, more than one bracket will be needed. When two brackets are required, it is vital that they are positioned perfectly level so that when the rail, or other accessory, is fitted in the brackets you achieve the best possible finish. In such instances, always use a spirit level to draw a horizontal pencil guideline along the tiles, and measure along this line to mark the exact positions where holes need to be drilled for the fixings. You can then use the drilling technique shown in steps 3 and 4. Once the holes have been made, rub out the pencil line with an eraser and then finish fixing the brackets in place. The way that accessories are inserted into the brackets varies between manufacturers, so always pay close attention to their specific instructions to ensure that all fixings are secure.

repairing a bathroom

Bathroom repairs fall into two categories: those concerned with fittings and the practical functions of the room, and those related to the various decorative aspects and overall appearance of the bathroom. Even the best-quality fittings or finishes will need repairs or maintenance at some stage, so it is worth being prepared for such occasions by learning in advance how to deal with the problems if they arise. This chapter considers the many repair issues associated with bathrooms and describes the best techniques for dealing with problems you are likely to encounter.

113

Replacing washers and re-enamelling the bath are just a few repairs that will keep this bathroom in working order.

fixing dripping taps ⤷⤷⤷

Dripping taps are a common problem but repairs are usually simple to carry out. Leaving a tap that is dripping is not only a waste of water but can also lead to stained fittings, so it is best to deal with the problem immediately. Although manufacturers regularly update tap designs, the way in which leaks and drips are repaired remains relatively unchanged. Rubber washers are the most common type of seal used in tap design – the more modern alternative is ceramic cartridges.

Rubber washers are situated at the base of the headgear deep inside the tap design. In order to gain access to the washer, you must disassemble the tap. There will always be slight variations in the dismantling procedure depending on the tap design. This usually relates to whether the tap handle is held in place with a retaining screw or simply push fit. Retaining screws may also be covered with caps, so gaining access to them may not be instantly obvious. The example below shows a common tap design and demonstrates the main principles of gaining access to washers and the way in which they are replaced.

Before beginning work, you will need to turn off water at the mains or by closing the shut-off valve below the relevant tap. Make sure that you allow any water left in the pipes to run off before dismantling. If you forget to do this, it will spill out when you remove the tap headgear from the tap body.

replacing washers

tools for the job

screwdriver

adjustable spanners

long-nose & slip-joint pliers

craft knife

1 Remove the tap handle. In this case, it simply pulls away from the main body of the tap.

2 Unscrew the retaining screw at the top of the plastic cover that is fitted over the tap headgear.

3 This cover acts purely as a mounting for the tap handle, so simply pull it off the headgear.

4 Use an adjustable spanner to undo the headgear from its position in the main tap body. You may need to clamp another spanner or some slip-joint pliers onto the tap body to hold it in place while you apply the necessary pressure to undo the headgear. If this extra support is required, either tape the jaws of the pliers or wrap a cloth around the tap body to prevent scratches.

5 With the headgear removed, you can gain access to the washer. In this case, it is secured in position with a nut. This can be removed with a pair of long-nose pliers or a small adjustable spanner, as shown here.

6 Remove the old washer. You will probably find it easiest to do this by using a slot-head screwdriver to flick it off. Replace it with a new washer before reassembling the tap.

tips of the trade

• **Avoiding losing parts** – Make sure the sink plug is in place when changing a washer, because the various small screws and parts of the tap can easily be dropped in the sink and disappear down the plughole.

• **Easing washers** – In many cases, the washer will not be held in place with a nut but simply pushed onto the end of the headgear. The old washer can be cut away using a craft knife if it is difficult to remove. Soaking the new washer in hot water can make it more pliable and easier to press into place.

OTHER TYPES OF LEAK

Replacing washers will deal with leaks from the spout of the tap. However, leaks that occur further up the tap body are more likely to be caused by the failure of a different type of seal. This seal is referred to as an O-ring and can be found in a number of places in the tap, on both the tap headgear and within some spout designs. If leaks become apparent around the shrouds that cover the tap headgear or at the base of the spout on a monobloc tap, the O-ring seal usually needs to be replaced.

replacing ceramic disc cartridges

This modern type of water-control system is very efficient and it is unusual to have to replace a disc cartridge because of leakage. In fact, it is so rare that there are no small parts such as washers that can be changed. Instead, the whole cartridge must be exchanged for a new one. There are many different designs of cartridge so it is important to know the correct type for your particular bathroom before purchase.

Before beginning work, make sure that the water is turned off at the mains or that the shut-off valve below the relevant tap has been closed. Run off any water left in the pipes before you start work.

tools for the job

screwdriver

adjustable spanners

1 Remove the tap handle. In this case, a cap is unscrewed off the top of the handle to gain access to the retaining screw below. The tap shroud can then be unscrewed. This will often come away by hand but adjustable spanners or pliers can be used if greater pressure is required. Protect the surface of the shroud to prevent it from being scratched, if using spanners or pliers.

2 Unscrew the cartridge from the main tap body using an adjustable spanner. You may need to grip the tap body in order to provide the necessary leverage.

3 Pull the old cartridge out of the tap body and replace it with a new one. The tap may now be reassembled.

OTHER TAP MECHANISMS

The repairs shown here relate to two different types of tap design. However, there are other mechanisms used to control water flow. Some modern taps are controlled with a ball-type mechanism in which one handle is used to control the flow of both the hot and cold taps. Washers and O-rings are still used in their design, however, so methods of repair are similar. There are sometimes small differences between designs from different manufacturers, who often produce specific repair kits for each type of tap.

dealing with shower problems ⚒

Showers can suffer disrepair to both their functioning and finish. In terms of finish, most repairs relate to the constant action of water hitting wall surfaces, combined with the humid atmosphere. Whether the shower is enclosed in a separate cubicle or positioned in a bath, steam can have a marked effect on surrounding painted surfaces. As far as function is concerned, there are a few simple maintenance procedures that will ensure the best performance from your shower.

installing a pvc ceiling

The ceiling directly above the shower is the area that suffers most from water damage. Moisture accumulates there and can lead to a breakdown of the decorated surface (normally paint). To prevent this, a sheet of pvc (polyvinyl chloride) can be fitted to form a totally waterproof area.

tools for the job

pencil

tape measure

panel saw

sealant gun or dispenser

1 Measure the dimensions of the ceiling area above your shower. For an enclosed shower, this will be the entire ceiling inside the cubicle – otherwise, you will have to judge what size area you need to cover.

2 Mark the dimensions on the sheet of pvc and cut it to size using a panel saw.

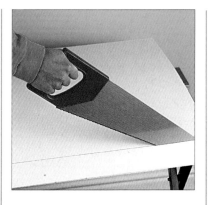

3 Apply a generous quantity of silicone sealant across the back of the pvc sheet.

4 Hold the sheet securely in place and the sealant should adhere quickly.

5 Once the sealant has dried, apply a further bead of silicone around the edge of the sheet to create a neat seal. You may wish to use masking tape to help you achieve a neat sealant line (see page 103). Once this has dried, the shower may be used. It is normally best to leave this last application of sealant to dry for 24 hours.

FIXING PVC WITH SCREWS

If the pvc sheet does not adhere easily to the ceiling, you may need to hold it in place with some sort of mechanical fixing. Drill pilot holes through the sheet and into the ceiling, then insert screws to hold it in position. Ideally, snap some pvc caps onto the screw heads to disguise them and make the sheet more pleasing to the eye. To ensure a good seal around the screws, apply a small quantity of sealant to the screw head before inserting it. In this way, as the screw is driven into place, the sealant wraps around the thread of the screw and creates a watertight seal.

painting the ceiling

Problems with peeling paint, build-up of mould and staining are often the result of the type of paint used and the fact that the area is not often wiped. Wear protective gloves when carrying out this process.

tools for the job

protective gloves

cloth or sponge

paintbrush

1 Sand the area, then wipe with a fungicidal solution to kill mould. Allow it to dry, then rinse with water.

2 Oil-based eggshell paint is more durable and resistant to moisture and condensation than standard emulsion paint (see also page 106 for the best paints to use in a bathroom). Apply two or three generous coats and allow to dry thoroughly.

maintenance

Many of the problems associated with shower fittings are related to the shower head itself or the hose. These elements of the shower are in frequent use, so regular maintenance should be undertaken.

head cleaning

Shower jet holes can often become blocked with limescale, and this is particularly true if you live in a hard-water area. If this happens, you should disassemble the head and descale the holes. Always wear protective gloves when handling descaling fluid.

tools for the job

screwdriver

toothbrush

protective gloves

1 The way in which shower heads are dismantled varies between manufacturers, but in most cases there is an obvious screw fitting that is simply undone in order to gain access to the inside of the shower head.

2 Clean the jet holes with a descaling fluid. Use an old toothbrush to apply the fluid to all of the intricate mouldings of the

shower head. Be sure to read the manufacturer's guidelines carefully for the solution you are using, and check that it is suitable for plastic- or metal-based shower heads.

tips of the trade

Some blockages in shower holes can be removed using a pin (although take care not prick yourself while doing so). However, you should avoid this method if your shower head contains plastic diaphragms because these can be damaged by the pin.

hose replacement

Another common problem with showers is when the hose begins to leak around the connection with the head itself. In some cases the problem can easily be fixed with a washer, but in general a new hose is required. Be sure to get the correct size of replacement hose, then simply unscrew the old one and screw the new one in place.

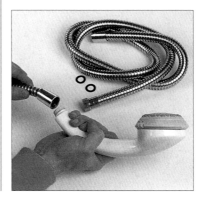

117

dealing with blockages & leaks

Many problems in bathrooms are hidden away from view but their effects can be devastating if not acted upon quickly. Blockages of any nature should be dealt with as soon as they are noticed, because any delay could lead to repairs that incur a much greater cost. Likewise, any leaking pipes should be repaired immediately because once water does begin to drip from a joint or hole, it will not stop unless an adequate repair is made.

simple basin solutions

There are two methods of dealing with basin blockages, both of which are outlined here.

using chemical cleaners

There are various chemical cleaners available. Most are caustic (generally containing sodium hydroxide) and, as such, protective gloves should always be worn. They are best used when the first signs of a blockage become apparent. Read the manufacturer's guidelines carefully, but in general one or two spoonfuls of the cleaner need to be poured into the plug hole in the basin. Run a small amount of water to ensure that none of the granules are allowed to rest on any exposed part of the sink bowl. Leave the cleaner to work for 20–30 minutes, before flushing the system with more water. One further application may be required to clear the blockage. Make sure there is adequate ventilation when carrying out this procedure because the fumes can be quite overpowering.

safety advice

For homes with a septic tank as part of their drainage system, chemical-based caustic cleaner cannot be used. Instead, a bacteria-based treatment must be employed. As usual, always follow the manufacturer's instructions.

using plungers

When chemical cleaners are ineffective, the next option to try is a plunger. First, you must create an airlock in the drainage system. This can be achieved by inserting a rag or cloth in the overflow outlet. When you have done this, position the suction pad of the plunger over the basin outlet. Move the plunger handle rhythmically up and down, which should put enough pressure on the blockage to loosen it. In this example, a modern design of plunger has been used that works on a similar principle to traditional designs except that water is sucked into the plunger cylinder and forced at high pressure into the blockage below, thereby dislodging it.

unblocking toilets

Toilets can be unblocked using a plunger in the same way that you would unblock a sink, as long as the head of the plunger is large enough to cover the outlet in the toilet pan. Alternatively, use an auger as demonstrated below.

1 Pull out the spring section of the auger to a suitable length for extending around the U-bend of the toilet.

2 Push the spring section into the U-bend of the toilet and turn the handle on the back.

supply pipe problems

When dealing with small leaks or drips on supply pipes, always consider the simple solutions before taking more drastic action. It is often the case that an extra turn with a spanner or the resealing of a joint will cure the problem.

compression joints

A leaking compression joint can often be fixed by turning the securing nuts one more time with some adjustable spanners. However, if a single turn does not cure the problem, it generally means that the joint itself has failed and needs replacing.

taping threads

Leaks on threaded joints can generally be cured by adding some ptfe (polytetrafluoroethylene) tape. Simply wind some tape around the threaded section of the joint before screwing it back into place.

replacing a section of pipe

A misplaced nail is a common cause of pipe leakages and dealing with the problem quickly is essential. Shut off the water supply to pipe first of all.

tools for the job

screwdriver

hacksaw

adjustable spanners

1 To stem the immediate flow from a punctured pipe, insert a screw into the puncture whose thread is slightly larger than the hole. A couple of turns of the screw can sometimes even seal the flow completely.

2 Once the water supply is switched off, use a hacksaw to cut out the section of pipe.

3 Dismantle a compression joint, slipping one section and the olive (small ring) onto the pipe on one side of the damaged area.

4 Repeat this process on the other side of the pipe, then cut a new section to fit between the two. Marry up the corresponding sections of each compression joint.

5 Tighten the joints using a pair of adjustable spanners.

tips of the trade

If the pipe you are repairing does not have enough flexibility so that the sections can be moved together and apart, use plastic pipe with appropriate adaptors (see pages 42–3).

119

repairing a bath ⚒

Baths can be given a new look by simply changing the panels or choosing a new design of tap to update the style. In addition, the actual bath surface can be repaired to hide scratches or defects as long as the correct materials and techniques are used. Proprietary re-enamelling kits are easy to apply and can make an old bathtub look like new. Replacing the sealant around the edges of the bath is also very effective in brightening up general bath appearance.

re-enamelling a bath

Although enamel baths are very hardwearing, they eventually tarnish, with their surface becoming stained or losing its enamel finish in places. A professional re-enamelling is an expensive business but there are now proprietary kits available that have some success returning old enamel baths to their original condition. They are easy to use but careful application is necessary to achieve a reasonable finish. Often these kits can be used on more than just enamel surfaces – sometimes ceramic, iron or plastic baths can be recoated using the same procedure, however the kits cannot be used on acrylic baths. Read the manufacturer's guidelines carefully to make sure that the kit is suitable for your particular bath surface. In this example, an old enamel bath is being renovated using one such proprietary kit.

tools for the job

sponge
cloth
proprietary re-enamelling kit
cordless drill/driver

1 First, clean any dirt or grime off the bath surface using a mild detergent and allow it to dry thoroughly. Cover the taps and waste outlets with masking tape or remove these items temporarily while re-enamelling takes place.

2 Clean the bath using the cleaner and sponge supplied with the kit. Rinse and allow to dry.

3 Sand the bath surface using fine-grade abrasive paper. Rinse with warm water and allow to dry.

safety advice

Make sure that the bathroom is adequately ventilated when using re-enamelling kits because the fumes can be quite overpowering.

4 Most kit systems involve mixing a hardener with the coating prior to application. Follow the manufacturer's guidelines.

5 Use a brush to paint all the detailed areas around outlets and taps, and generally those places where a roller would be unable to gain access. Take care to apply the coating as evenly as possible.

6 Pour some of the coating mixture into a roller tray or the tray supplied with the kit, and distribute the coating evenly over the roller surface.

7 Apply the coating to the bath as evenly as possible, reloading the roller at appropriate intervals. Try to cover any unsightly brushmarks.

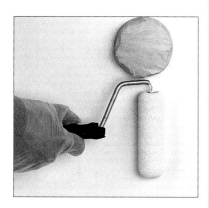

8 Once the coating is dry, apply another coat. Again, try to cover previous brushmarks and roller marks in order to produce an even finish. When the surface is dry, remove the masking tape.

tips of the trade

• **Sealant removal –** Where the bath is in contact with wall surfaces, be sure to remove any sealant so that the new coating extends right up to the edge.

• **Drying time –** Coatings may need to dry for 48 hours before the bath can be used, so make sure you read the manufacturer's guidelines for any specific instructions.

• **Future cleaning –** After the bath has been coated, only use liquid, non-abrasive cleaners on its surface, applied with a sponge or cloth.

• **Further protection –** As a further protective measure, apply a coat of car wax to the bath once or twice a year to help maintain its finish and keep it as clean and bright as possible.

• **Change sleeves –** Use a different roller sleeve for each coating because it is not possible to clean the roller between coats. If you attempt to use the same roller sleeve for the second coat it will produce a very rough and unsatisfactory finish.

DISGUISING SCRATCHES

Small scratches or chips on what is otherwise an acceptable bath surface finish can be disguised by dabbing a small amount of oil-based eggshell paint onto the mark. Remove any excess with a cloth and allow it to dry before using the bath.

replacing seals

The sealant around the edge of a bath will need to be repaired at some point during the lifetime of the bath. Removing the old seal and replacing it with a new one is a simple process.

tools for the job

small paintbrush

window scraper

sealant gun or dispenser

1 Use a small paintbrush to apply a proprietary sealant removal solution along the sealant bead. Allow this to soak into the sealant according to the manufacturer's guidelines.

2 Use a window scraper to ease the sealant away from the wall and bath surface, taking care not to scratch the surface of the bath.

3 Use a cloth to clean away any remaining sealant. Dampening the cloth with methylated spirits will help to prepare the surface for reapplication of sealant (follow the steps for 'sealing' on page 103).

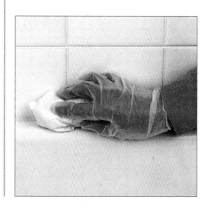

making tile repairs ⚒

It is almost inevitable that the tiles in a bathroom will become damaged and that their appearance will deteriorate over time. Rather than completely retiling, you may prefer to carry out some sort of repair or renovation to restore a good finish to the existing tiled surface. The degree of damage may vary in seriousness, from broken or cracked tiles to simple grout discoloration. Whatever the damage done, carrying out a repair is a relatively straightforward process.

Condensation, general moisture levels, and wear and tear over time, are all factors that contribute to the gradual deterioration of grout joints between tiles. Often the main reason people choose to change tiles in their bathroom is because the old grout has become discoloured and detracts from the overall appearance of the tiled surface. However, it is not always necessary to retile and often tiles can look good as new by either reviving or replacing the grout.

regrouting

tools for the job

grout raker
vacuum cleaner
grout spreader
sponge

1 Employ a specially designed grout raker to remove old grout from joints. The serrated, roughened edge digs out the grout as you apply pressure to the surface. Take care not to scratch the edge of the tiles.

2 Once you have raked out all the joints from around the tiles, it is important to remove any dust or debris from both the tile surface and within the joints. Wipe the surface down and use a vacuum cleaner to remove debris from the tile joints.

3 With the old grout completely removed from the joints, regrout the tiles using the usual techniques (see page 103). However, for a slightly different look you might like to consider using a coloured grout as a change to the standard white varieties. Grout colouring is usually supplied in a powdered form, which is mixed with white grout until the desired colour intensity is achieved.

grout reviver

Reviving grout is in many ways a simpler and quicker way of restoring grout to a clean finish when compared to regrouting. Total regrouting does tend to last longer and is the more hardwearing option, but because the task of grout revival is quick, it can be performed on a more regular basis. Grout reviver tends to be supplied in proprietary kit form.

tools for the job

grout reviving kit
sponge

Make sure the tile surface has been thoroughly cleaned and is completely dry. Apply the reviver along all the grout joints in the same way that you would apply paint. Wipe away any excess reviver using a damp sponge. There is normally a critical timing between application and wiping away excess, so you should always refer to the manufacturer's guidelines in order to attain the best finish.

replacing a tile

Tiles can be broken by accident, or they can simply crack over time due to weaknesses in their manufacture. Whatever the reason, the process for replacing a broken tile is the same. It can be difficult to find an exact match for the tile being replaced and even small colour variations are noticeable in the finished product, so choose carefully. This is a good reason for always holding onto a few tiles when you finish any new tiling project.

tools for the job

cordless drill/driver

scraper

club hammer

cold chisel

protective gloves

goggles

adhesive spreader

grout spreader

sponge

safety advice

When drilling into tiles and removing them, always wear goggles to protect your eyes from any flying debris.

1 Drill a number of holes into the broken tile surface to weaken its structure. Use a tile drill bit if possible, but since accuracy is not paramount a masonry bit should break through

the tile just as well. Make sure the drill does not slip onto surrounding tiles and risk damaging them.

2 The next step is to loosen the grout around the edge of the broken tile with a grout raker.

3 Remove the damaged tile with a club hammer and cold chisel. Again, take care to position the point of the chisel so that it cannot slip and damage the surrounding tiles.

4 Use a scraper to remove any remaining tile adhesive from the wall surface.

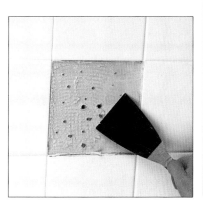

5 Apply adhesive to the space left by the old tile and position the new one. Use spacers to maintain a consistent gap around the edge of the tile for the grouting joints. The spacers will have to be applied at right angles to the tile surface.

6 Hold a batten across the tile surface to check that the new tile sits flush with the surrounding tiles. If necessary, adjust adhesive levels until the tile sits flush.

7 Once the adhesive has dried, remove the spacers and grout the tile joints in the usual way.

123

renovating an existing bathroom

You do not have to replace a bathroom completely in order to change its overall appearance. If you are happy with your existing suite and merely wish to update the look of the room, there are a number of ways in which a change of decorative emphasis can transform it into something that matches your present aspirations. This chapter considers those renovations that only require selective changes. Each of the examples discussed can be tailored to meet your specific needs and adjusted to account for personal taste and preference.

With a bright painting scheme and decorative tiling, this bathroom has been given a whole new look.

changing lighting

Lighting is particularly important in bathrooms if you wish to create a relaxing ambience. The range of options available is huge, and manufacturers are continually making innovations in terms of both function and design. As well as selecting an appropriate type of fitting, you also need to appreciate the effect that light has on other items in the room, such as mirrors. Wiring and connection of electrical fittings must always be undertaken by a professional electrician.

flush lighting

Flush light fittings are lights recessed into a ceiling or wall so that they are level with its surface. Flush lighting is increasing in popularity because of its neat, modern look and the effectiveness of the light produced. Many such fittings are low voltage and provide a soft ambience in the bathroom, ideal for relaxation. Several lights are usually installed to provide adequate illumination in all areas of the room without the harshness of an overhead pendant light.

RIGHT *Flush lighting enhances the look of a sleek, modern bathroom and, because it gives off a soft light that can be adjusted to fall in different directions, it offers the perfect 'mood' lighting to create a relaxing atmosphere.*

BELOW *In this bathroom a flush light fitting has been installed directly above the shower cubicle to illuminate an area where pendant lighting is inappropriate. This in turn has enabled the cubicle to be boxed in to create a handy wall surface upon which the toilet roll holder and magazine rack may be fixed.*

LIGHTING RAILS

Rail-mounted lights are another modern innovation perfect for a contemporary bathroom. The intricate nature of lighting rails makes them an excellent design feature, and many systems allow the lights to be moved along the rails so that the direction and emphasis of the light can be changed. Again, these systems are often low voltage and as such provide a soft, even distribution of light.

low-level lighting

Low-level or wall lighting is usually found in more traditional bathrooms, where elegant and decorative features shape the look of the room, but it can also be adapted to modern design. This type of lighting system is directional in nature and as such produces different amounts of light in each area of the room and creates strong lighting contrasts in the room as a whole. This directional lighting is ideal for creating good illumination in working areas such as around basins, so that using the bathroom for specific functions is made as easy as possible.

mirrors

Mirrors fulfil both an aesthetic and functional purpose, since their reflective properties can help to increase the illumination of the bathroom even if light sources are limited. This has the added bonus of creating a greater feeling of space within the room. Size will play an important role – the larger the mirror, the greater the reflective effect.

ABOVE RIGHT *Flush lights have been fitted with directional covers and installed in a wall to create stylish and practical low-level lighting above the sink area.*

RIGHT *Specific lighting systems designed for use with mirrors provide great decorative impact and make using the mirror as easy and effective as possible.*

BELOW *The limited natural light source in this bathroom is enhanced by using pale colours in the decoration and fittings to reflect and draw as much light into the room as possible.*

natural light

Choosing wall colours, suites and tiles to reflect the natural light in the bathroom can help to make a dark room appear much lighter and airier. Clearly the degree of success here will depend on the amount of natural light the room receives, but appreciating how to use the light available can help to shape the atmosphere of the room as a whole.

building a glass block wall ↗↗↗

Glass block walls make fine decorative additions to a bathroom, forming partitions or even shower cubicles, although they should not be used for any structural purposes. They can be constructed using either a wooden framework or the more traditional method of mortaring. In the latter case it is best to use a special white mortar to make the jointing look as attractive as possible. When planning a wall, remember that glass blocks cannot be cut and so measurements must account for whole blocks ending in the required positions.

using a framework

Proprietary kits are available for glass block wall systems that can quickly be assembled with the minimum of mess. This type of wall should not be used where waterproofing is essential (in a shower cubicle for example), but rather as a simple dividing partition.

tools for the job

pencil
tape measure
spirit level
mitresaw or panel saw
cordless drill/driver
screwdriver

1 Having decided on wall position, check the wall plate is precisely vertical with a spirit level. Clips on the wall plate for joining the horizontal sections should already have been installed by the manufacturer. You may need to cut down the height of the wall plate to the required level.

2 Fix the wall plate in position with wall plugs and screws or, as shown here, with concrete anchors inserted directly into a solid block wall. Ensure that the screw heads sit flush on the wall plate surface, as any protrusions may cause the glass blocks to be positioned imprecisely. Continue to check the vertical position of the wall plate as fixings are added.

3 Clip the sole plate in position at the base of the wall plate, hooking it in place so that it extends at a precise 90° angle from the wall. Firmly screw the sole plate to the floor using concrete anchors for solid floors or simple screws for wooden floors

(as shown here). Make sure the screws do not penetrate so far that they risk damaging underfloor services.

4 Position the first glass block on the sole plate and slide it into place at the base of the wall plate. The wall and sole plates exhibit a channel design that holds the glass block loosely in position.

5 Position a vertical strut next to the glass block to provide a barrier, then add the next block. The struts require no physical fixings as the weight of the blocks alone will hold them in place. Continue adding blocks and struts along the row.

6 Once the bottom row of blocks is complete, you will need to add a horizontal strut to provide the base for the next row. If these horizontal struts have not already been cut to size by the manufacturer, cut them to the correct dimensions with a mitresaw or panel saw. Screw the necessary attachments into the ends of the struts for linking them to the wall plates.

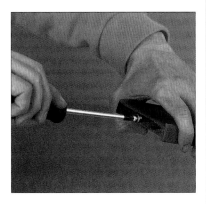

7 Position the horizontal strut on top of the row of blocks and clip it into the wall plate, checking that it sits level. This is also a good point to check the horizontal level of the block wall. If any adjustments are needed this can be done by building up the level of the sole plate, so that as further rows of blocks are added, the overall structure remains precisely vertical and correctly positioned.

8 After positioning the top row of blocks, add a head plate to act as the finishing section on top of the wall. Finally, add another wall plate to the open end of the block wall.

using mortar

tools for the job

pencil
tape measure
nail & line
spirit level
hammer
cordless drill/driver
gauging trowel
sponge

Using mortar to build a glass block wall requires some aptitude for applying mortar and laying blocks level. Spacers help to maintain the distance between blocks both on the same row and between levels. You will need to position the first row with a string line and frequently check for position with a spirit level.

1 Draw a vertical line on the wall, then extend a string line to the opposite wall that corresponds to the height of the first row of blocks. Steel

rods are used to strengthen the block wall. Place a block 'dry', mark off the position and drill a hole for the first rod into the wall at this mark.

2 Position the first block with spacers then apply mortar to the area between the spacers. Butter the end of the block with mortar before positioning it against the wall and bedding it down into the mortar base.

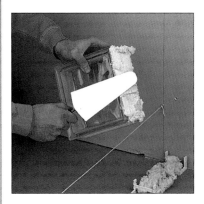

3 Continue to add blocks, spacers and steel bars on each course. (You can also add steel bars vertically through joints as the wall is built up.) Once complete, remove spacer face plates, then grout and polish to finish.

WALL BASE

Glass block walls may be built on either concrete or timber floors. On concrete floors, apply blocks directly to the floor surface with either mortar or a framework. On wooden floors, the framework provides all the support needed, but if using mortar, fix a wooden sole plate for extra support.

fitting tongue & groove panelling ✂✂

The use of tongue and groove panelling is an extremely effective way of transforming a wall surface and making a bathroom feel warm and inviting. The panelling can be applied across entire walls or just up to dado level, as in the example demonstrated here. Applying panelling is a two-part process – first you need to build a framework onto which the boards will be applied, then you must cut the boards to fit the space and fix them in place.

safety advice

Always check for hidden cables or supply pipes with a pipe and cable detector before drilling into walls to fix the battens and panelling in place.

tools for the job

pencil
tape measure
spirit level
panel saw
cordless drill/driver
hammer
nail punch
mitresaw

building the framework

Tongue and groove panelling should be attached to a batten framework. Although 5 x 2.5cm (2 x 1in) battens are often ideal, it can be advantageous to use slightly larger battens such as 5 x 5cm (2 x 2in) in bathrooms so that a shelf can be formed across the top of the panelling for extra storage. Another advantage is that they produce deep panelling, which means that pipes attached to the wall can often run beneath the framework.

1 A good height for dado panelling is approximately 1m (1yd) above floor level. For these dimensions, three horizontal battens should be fixed to the wall surface, one at floor level, one at the required height for the top of the panelling and one about halfway between the two. Draw guidelines for these battens using a spirit level to make sure that they are horizontal.

2 Fix the battens to the wall surface using the guidelines for positioning. In this case, concrete anchors are inserted directly through the battens into the masonry wall below. For hollow walls, use the correct wall plugs and screw fixings to hold the battens in place.

3 To deal with any pipes, cut batten lengths so that a gap is left to allow the pipe to run down through the framework.

attaching the panelling

The structure of tongue and groove panelling allows it to be fitted in place so that the actual fixing points are hidden from view. In simple terms, small nails or panel pins (depending on the thickness of the panelling) are inserted at 45° angles through the tongue of a board to hold it in place. The groove of the next board covers this tongue and, therefore, the fixing. When applying boards it is best to start at an internal corner and have a number of boards cut to size before you begin so that progress is swift. However, be aware of the fact that small undulations or slopes in the floor may mean that you need different heights of board if the top of the panelling is to be neat and level.

tips of the trade

Remember to make access hatches in the panelling for any stopcocks or shut-off valves, so that the water supply can be turned off easily in an emergency (see page 63).

1 Position the first board using a spirit level to check that it is completely vertical.

2 Fix the first board to the battens through the top, middle and bottom of its face. Only hidden fixings should be necessary with all subsequent boards.

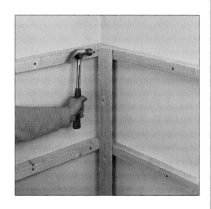

3 Knock nails through the tongue of the board and use a nail punch to make sure that the head disappears below wood surface level.

tips of the trade

• **Selective panelling** – On walls that have a number of fittings such as a basin, bidet and toilet, building a framework and panelling can be a complicated procedure. It is often worth panelling only those walls that are relatively free from obstacles.

• **Decoration** – Tongue and groove panelling can be finished with paint or coated with a natural wood stain or varnish to complement the existing decoration in the room.

4 Keep adding boards, slipping the groove of the new length over the tongue of the previous one, and inserting nails along the tongue of the new board.

5 You will need to add a decorative moulding at external corners to cover the joint. This can either be glued or nailed in position.

6 To finish the top of the panelling, cut some 7.5 x 2.5cm (3 x 1in) batten, mitring the joints neatly at the corners. This produces a much more attractive and professional finish than butting the straight edges.

7 Fix the 7.5 x 2.5cm (3 x 1in) batten in place by inserting screws or nails through the batten into the 5 x 5cm (2 x 2in) batten below to secure it in position.

8 Add a decorative moulding around the underside of the 7.5 x 2.5cm (3 x 1in) batten for a more attractive result.

ALTERNATIVE EDGING

Instead of using moulding, you can achieve a simpler finish by routing the edge of the top batten.

half-tiling a bathroom ⁄⁄⁄

Many people assume that a fully tiled bathroom in need of renovation must be stripped of all the tiles before any changes can be made. However, as long as the existing tiles are securely fixed to the wall surface, there is nothing to stop you from using them as the base for new decoration. It may be possible to tile completely over the old surface or, as shown in this example, change the room from being fully tiled to half-tiled.

tools for the job

pencil & tape measure

spirit level

cordless drill/driver

paintbrush

power drill & mixing attachment

plastering trowel

notched spreader

tile cutter

grout spreader

sponge

1 This procedure involves applying new tiles to half the wall and plastering over the remaining old tiles. You need to create a dividing line between the two areas, using a wooden dado rail or moulding fixed in place approximately 1m (1yd) above floor level. Use a spirit level to draw a horizontal guideline on the wall. You will probably need to use a tile drill bit to make pilot holes in the tile surface for attaching the rail. Use concrete anchor screws if it is a solid masonry wall, or the appropriate wall plugs and standard screw fixings for a hollow wall.

2 Clean the tile surface above the dado rail. Allow it to dry, then sand it to provide a key for the new surface finish. Apply a coat of pva (polyvinyl adhesive) solution to the tiles (50:50 water and pva), allowing the coat to become tacky before you begin to apply plaster.

3 Mix some plaster and apply it across the area above the dado rail using a plastering trowel (refer to 'tips of the trade', above right, for advice on mixing and applying plaster to achieve the best possible finish). Press the plaster firmly onto the wall surface using wide, sweeping strokes with the blade of the trowel to achieve a smooth result.

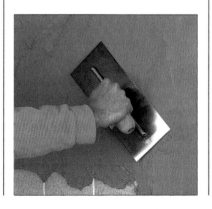

tips of the trade

• **Mixing plaster** – Use multi-finish plaster and mix it into a smooth, creamy consistency. If possible, use a power drill with a mixing attachment to aid the process.

• **Polishing** – Once the plaster has been applied to the wall surface and smoothed to the best of your ability, allow it to dry to a firm but still wet-to-the-touch finish. You can then polish the plaster with a dampened plastering trowel to smooth out any surface imperfections.

• **Drying time** – Plaster that is applied over tiles rather than plasterboard will take longer to dry than usual. Do not be tempted to apply any paint or paper before the newly plastered walls have completely dried.

4 Plan the design of the new tiles below the dado rail so that their joints do not coincide with those of the old tile design. A row of full tiles at the top will always provide the best finished look. Measure down from the dado rail and mark on the first row of tiles, which should be positioned a distance above the skirting that allows you to finish with a row of full tiles.

5 Screw a supporting batten into the wall above the skirting board to provide a base for the first row of tiles. As in step 1, use the appropriate fixings to hold the batten in place. You may need to use a tile bit to break through the surface of the tiles.

6 Apply adhesive over the old tiles with a notched spreader. Position the new tiles, using spacers in the usual way (see also pages 100–3).

7 Continue building up the rows of tiles, finishing the design below the dado rail with a row of full tiles, as planned.

8 Leave the tiles to dry. The adhesive will take longer than usual to dry due to the old tile base. It is best to wait 48 hours before proceeding. Once they are dry, you can remove the supporting batten and fill the area beneath it with cut tiles. When the adhesive for the cut tiles has dried, grout the entire surface in the usual way and wipe the area clean with a damp sponge. See pages 102–3 for how to cut tiles.

ALTERNATIVE EDGINGS

A half-tiled bathroom does not have to be finished with a wooden dado rail along its top edge. You could attach a plastic trim to the wall with adhesive at the required height and butt the tiles into its edge. Alternatively, apply border tiles. The relief design of the tiles used in this example also helps to produce a more three-dimensional effect.

A row of patterned tiles in this half-tile design provide an attractive dividing line in the wall surface, and it is particularly effective in high-ceiling rooms.

adding to existing tiles ⚒

Another way of changing the look of your bathroom is to make additions or slight alterations to the existing tile layout. In many instances, even if tiles still look new and bright, a slight update in appearance can work wonders. The examples shown here should only be carried out on sound existing tile surfaces. If tiles are coming away from the wall or are poorly fitted, then you should remove the old ones and begin from scratch (see also pages 122–3 for how to remove tiles).

tile transfers

A bank of clean white tiles may look good in some bathrooms, but using tile transfers to add pattern to a bland tile surface can be an attractive option if you wish to brighten up the room. The exact method of application can vary slightly between manufacturers but the principles of soaking and positioning transfers remains similar.

tools for the job

sponge

bucket

cloth

1 The first job is to make sure that the tile surface is completely clean by wiping away all traces of dirt or grime with a sponge.

2 Soak the transfer in a bucket of clean warm water making sure that the entire sheet is immersed. Read the manufacturer's guidelines for the required soaking time.

3 Remove the transfer from the bucket and shake off excess water. Position the transfer on the tile.

4 When happy with the position, slide off the backing paper to leave the transfer image on the tile.

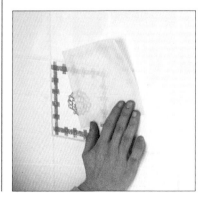

tips of the trade 👍

Do not position transfers in areas that are prone to abrasion. Although they are fairly robust once dry, they cannot withstand regular rigorous cleaning. It is a good idea to buy a few extra transfers so that you can replace any that may get damaged, although this problem will not arise if you choose to apply a selection of designs.

5 Dab the image with a dry cloth to remove excess water and smooth away air bubbles.

painting tiles

A simple way of changing tile appearance is to paint them a new colour or a combination of colours. Tile primers are now available that make this process possible and allow a durable finish to be achieved.

tools for the job

sponge

paintbrush

1 Sand the tiled surface to provide a key for the paint. Clean any dust or grime with a mild detergent and rinse with clean warm water. Allow the surface to dry completely.

2 Paint tile primer over the entire tiled surface. When dry, you can apply your chosen emulsion, eggshell or gloss paint.

👍
tips of the trade
If you use emulsion paint, varnish over the top to increase its durability.

adding picture tiles

Another way to liven up an existing area of tiles is to remove some of them and replace them with picture or patterned tiles. The technique for removing tiles is shown in more detail on pages 122–123, where broken tiles are removed before new ones are put in their places.

tools for the job

grout raker
cordless drill/driver
protective gloves & goggles
club hammer
cold chisel
notched spreader
grout spreader

1 Use a grout raker to scrape away as much grout as possible from around the edges of the tiles that are to be removed. Drill a number of holes through the surface of the tiles to weaken their structure, then use a club hammer and cold chisel to knock out the broken sections of tile. Remember to wear protective gloves and goggles.

2 Apply adhesive to the wall and press the new tile into position. Use spacers to maintain the gap around its edge while the adhesive dries. When completely dry, remove the spacers and grout the joints.

tile sheets

A quick, inexpensive way of changing the appearance of a tiled surface is to use plastic tile sheets. These are easy to apply and can be used over existing tile surfaces.

tools for the job

notched spreader
scissors
grout spreader

1 Use a notched spreader to apply adhesive to the back of the sheets making coverage as even as possible.

2 Press the sheets into position. The number of tiles on each sheet means that a large area can be covered very quickly. The sheets can be cut with scissors to fill in gaps around the edge of a design. Once the adhesive has dried, apply grout.

glossary

Access hatch – section cut out of boxing and made into hinged door or removable panel so that access may be gained behind the panel.

Air brick – brick containing a number of holes and used for ventilation in exterior bathroom walls.

Bath panel – decorative panel attached to side of bath, which is normally removable so that access may be gained under the bath.

Batten – thin pieces of wood used for boxing in and for sundry other construction requirements

Boxing in – technique of employing a framework to cover up unsightly items, such as pipes. Composed of wooden batten and covered with building board such as mdf.

Caulk – flexible filler supplied in a tube and dispensed from a sealant gun. Must be smoothed to finish before it dries.

Carcass – the basic structure of a bathroom unit where no embellishments such as doors or drawer fronts have been added.

Cavity wall – wall composed of two layers. In effect, two walls separated by a cavity or void. Common in the construction of external walls of modern homes.

Cistern – water storage tank for entire house supply or term applied to smaller tanks such as those used to supply a toilet.

Colourizer – concentrated colour supplied in small tubes or containers, designed to add colour to paint or scumble for paint effect purposes.

Some are universal in that they can be added to both acrylic and solvent based paints or glazes.

Concrete anchor – screw designed to fix into masonry without the need for a wall plug.

Connector – section of pipe used to connect other pipes.

Cornice – decorative moulding fixed around bottom edge of bathroom wall units, or decorative moulding fitted along wall/ceiling junction.

Dado rail – wooden rail or moulding denoting the top of the dado and therefore dividing up the wall surface into a lower and upper area. Sometimes referred to as a chair rail.

Dummy drawer front – drawer front that is not attached to a drawer but is fixed to a unit carcass to imitate

drawer position in order to maintain the decorative finish of a run of units.

Eggshell – hardwearing paint that has a dull matt finish. Available in acrylic or solvent-based forms.

Emulsion – acrylic or water-based paint used for open areas such as walls and ceilings.

Enamel – hardwearing decorative coating for bathroom fittings, traditionally used on old iron baths.

End panel – decorative panel attached to the side of wall or base units at the end of a run of units. Often matches finish of door fronts.

En-suite – term normally applied to a bathroom that is directly adjacent to and serving one particular room. En-suite rooms are normally created through building a stud partition wall in a larger room to provide space.

Fitted – of a bathroom that comprises similar units fixed permanently in position, usually integrated in 'runs'.

Floor unit – a bathroom unit that is installed at floor level.

Flush – where two or more surfaces create a seamless join.

Flush lighting – lighting systems that are recessed into a surface, such as sunken spotlights on a ceiling.

Flux – cleaning material used on joints prior to soldering.

Fan – mechanical ventilation system either ceiling or wall-mounted.

Gloss – highly decorative, hardwearing and shiny paint finish.

Grout – waterproof compound that fills the gap between tile joints.

Hard tile – ceramic wall or floor tiles as opposed to softer varieties such as cork or vinyl.

Hardboard – thin building board often used on floors to provide smooth subfloor below further floor covering.

Headgear – term denoting the internal mechanism of a tap.

Joist – length of wood used in the construction of ceilings and floors.

Joist detector – sensor device used for finding the position of joists in ceilings or walls. Some may also have a different mode that can be employed to trace the position of electric cables or pipes, hence it is an important safety tool to help avoid drilling or nailing into pipes and cables.

Laminate – term used to describe the process whereby a thin plastic layer is bonded to another surface, such as fibreboard, to create a bathroom worktop.

Lighting rails – lighting system where a number of lights are positioned along a rail – light position is generally adjustable along the length of the rail

Low-level lighting – lighting system where lighting position is well below ceiling level.

Mdf – or medium density fibreboard – building board made from compressed wooden fibres.

Mitre – angled joint, normally involving two lengths of material joining at a right angle, hence each piece must be cut at a 45° angle.

Monobloc – tap comprising one spout where hot and cold water is mixed to provide the required temperature.

Outlet pipe – waste pipe leading from a particular bathroom fitting trap into the drainage system.

Pedestal basin – a basin that is partially supported by a pedestal.

Pelmet – decorative moulding that is fixed around the bottom edge of bathroom wall units.

Plinth – board attached between the underside of base units and the floor in order to create a decorative finish, often clipped onto the feet of units using special brackets.

Pop-up waste – where plug for waste outlet is connected to the waste system, and is positioned in or removed from the waste outlet through the operation of a connecting rod or cable.

Proprietary – referring to a material, tool or technique that relates specifically to one manufacturer or group of manufacturers.

Ptfe – or polytetrafluoroethylene tape used for mending leaking joints.

Pva – short for polyvinyl acetate, all-purpose adhesive that may also be used diluted with water to form a stabilising solution for powdery wall, ceiling and floor surfaces.

Pvc – short for polyvinyl chloride.

Rim-supply – bidet design where water is supplied around and under the rim of the bidet with the purpose of warming the seat.

Scribing block – small piece of wood cut to a size that helps to mark off the trimming requirement on a section of worktop or panelling, so that it may be cut to a precise size.

Self-levelling compound – compound applied to concrete floors in order to provide a level surface for further floor covering.

Shower mixer – type of bath fitting where taps are directly connected to a shower hose and head, thereby producing a multi-purpose fitting.

Silicone sealant – waterproof sealant used along junctions.

Skirting board – decorative wooden moulding applied at base of wall.

Soft tile – decorative tiles made from pliable materials such as cork or vinyl.

Soil pipe – large diameter waste pipe into which waste from toilet is expelled, normally positioned on exterior wall of house.

Solvent-based or oil-based – terms used when referring to the make up of paint or glaze.

Solvent cement – adhesive for joining some designs of plastic waste pipe.

Spacers – plastic dividers placed between ceramic tiles to maintain consistency of distance between each of the tiles.

Splashback – area on wall surface directly above basins, baths or worktops, which has been covered over with an easily wipeable material, such as tiles.

Split level – where a room has a step in either floor or ceiling levels.

Static vent – ventilation grill with no mechanical parts.

Steam stripper – machine used to aid wallpaper stripping by expelling steam onto the wall surface, which causes the paper to bubble so that it can be removed more easily.

Stud – wooden uprights used in the construction of a stud wall.

Stud wall – wall consisting of wooden studs and covered in plasterboard. Used as non-load-bearing partition wall in houses.

Subfloor – the base floor material beneath a floor covering, usually either wooden floorboards or chipboard, or concrete.

Tongue and groove – interlocking mechanism used to join some types of planking, building or panelling board.

Traps – area directly below drainage outlet where waste is typically directed through a u-shaped section of pipe.

Unfitted – term used to describe bathroom layout where units are not permanently fixed in position.

Vinyl – manufactured substance used to produce decorative, easy-to-clean floor coverings. Also, protective covering on some wallpapers or additive used in paint, to improve their hardwearing and wipeable properties.

Vinyl emulsion – water based paint ideal for a bathroom environment as it contains vinyl and is therefore easier to wipe down and keep clean.

Wall plug – plastic or metal sheath, inserted into pre-drilled hole in wall to house screw.

Wall units – bathroom cabinets mounted on wall surfaces.

Washer – rubber rings that prevent water leaking from joints within taps.

Window dressing – decorative finish for windows e.g. curtains and blinds.

Wood glue – adhesive for joining together wooden sections.

Wall-mounted basin – basin mounted directly onto wall with bracket fixings, rather than with screws and resting on a pedestal.

Worktop – work surface positioned on top of fitted bathroom units.

index

mirror screws, 53, 77
mirror tiles, 77
mirrors, 25, 67, 76–7, 127
mixing concrete, 82
mobile storage, 66
monobloc taps, 46, 56
mortar, 129
mosaic floor tiles, 94–5
mould, fungicide, 117
mouldings, quadrant, 93

n
natural light, 127
noggings, 48, 58

o
O-rings, taps, 115
order of work, 32–3
overflows, baths, 51
over-rim supply bidets, 56

p
paint and painting, 99, 106
   ceilings, 117
   equipment, 106
   tiles, 134–5
panelling, tongue-and-groove, 130–1
panels, baths, 15, 52–3
pedestal basins, 27, 47
pelmets, blinds, 109
picture tiles, 135
pipe clips, 43
pipe cutters, 40
pipes and pipework, 19
   see also water supply
plumbing
   access, 25
   boxing in, 15, 62
   connectors see joints
   copper plumbing, 40–1
   cutting and joining, 40–1, 42
   drainage, 19
   gate valves, 7, 38, 43, 57, 63
   heated towel rails, 68–9
   joints, see joints
   leaks, 119
   overflows, baths, 51
plastic plumbing, 42–3

reducers, 43
rerouting pipes, 48, 69
shut-off valves, 7, 38, 43, 57, 63
soil pipes, toilets, 55
stop ends, 43
stopcocks, 7, 38, 43, 57, 63
   pipes, 43
   traps, 19, 57
   waste pipes, 39, 56
planning, 7, 12–13, 24
   see also preparation
   budgeting, 33
   disposal of old fixtures, 33
   laminate flooring, 92
   manufacturers' planning service, 25
   order of work, 32
   practical considerations, 24
   professionals, dealing with 32
   sanding floorboards, 90
   scale plans, 24-5
   tiling, 86, 100
   timescales, 33
plans, scale, 24–5
plasterboard, 48, 49, 58
plastering, 132–3
plastic membranes, 93
plastic pipes, cutting and joining, 41, 42–3
pliers, 34, 35
plinths, 14
plumbers, 32
plumbing, 7, 19
   see also pipes and pipework, water supply
   copper plumbing, 40–1
   plastic, 42–3
   preparation, 40–1
   tools, 35
plungers, 35, 118
polishing plaster, 132
pop-up waste outlets:
   basins, 46–7
   baths, 50–1
   bidets, 56
power showers, 30, 31
power tools, 35
   jigsaws, 83
   masonry drills, 71
   sanders, 90–1
   steam strippers, 107

tile cutters, 102
preparation, 38–9
   see also planning electrics, 41
   floorboards, 83
   plumbing, 40–1
   subfloors, 82–3
prices, 32
priming subfloors, 88
professionals, dealing with, 32
ptfe (polytetrafluoroethylene) tape, 35, 119
pva solution, 82, 88
pvc ceilings, 116

q
quadrant mouldings, 93
quotations, 32

r
rails, lighting, 126
re-enamelling baths, 120–1
recessed shower units, 58
reducers, 43
repairs and renovation, 8
   baths, 120–1
   blockages and leaks, 118–9
   dripping taps, 114–5
   showers, 116–7
   tiles, 122–3
rerouting:
   electrics, 41
   pipes, 48, 69
roll-top baths, 16, 26
roller blinds, 108
roman blinds, 108
routers, 35

s
safety:
   drilling tiles, 123
   electric towel rails, 68
   gas torches, 41
   hidden cables and pipes, 130
   medicine cabinets, 74
   mixing concrete, 82
   pipes and wiring, 110
   protective gloves, 105
   septic tanks, 118

water supply, 38
sanders, electric, 35, 90–1
sanding, floorboards, 90–1
saws, 34, 35
scale plans, 24–5
scratches, disguising, 121
screeds, concrete, 82
screens, bath, 59
screens, shower, types of, 31
screwdrivers, 34
screws, mirror screws, 77
sealants, 86, 89 see also silicone sealants
seals, replacing, 121
self-adhesive floor tiles, 88–9
self-levelling compound, 82
septic tanks, 118
shelves, 29, 66, 72–3, 130
shower screens, 31
shower trays and cubicles, 13, 31, 60-1
shower units, recessed, 58
showers:
   ceiling problems, 116–7
   drainage outlets, 31
   fungicide, 117
   head cleaning, 117
   hose replacement, 117
   installation, 58
   spray functions, 30
   types of, 30
   water supply, 58
shut-off valves, 7, 38, 57
   access, 63
   fitting 43
silicone sealant:
   bath panels, 85
   dispensers, 34
   flooring, 85
   removal, 121
   showers, 61
   splashbacks, 105
   wall tiles, 103
   wallpaper, 107
   waste outlets, 46, 51, 56
siphon units, 54
skirting boards, 52–3
soil pipes, toilets, 55
solder ring joints, 40–1
solvent weld cement, 41
space saving, 13, 27
splashbacks, tiling, 104–5
steam strippers, 107

useful contacts

suppliers

The authors and publisher would like to thank the following companies:

Armitage Shanks Limited
Armitage
Rugeley
Staffordshire
WS15 4BT
Tel. 0800 866966
www.armitage-shanks.co.uk

B.J. White
4 Vale Road
Pen Mill Trading Estate .
Yeovil
Somerset
BA21 5HL
Tel. 01935 382400

Bliss (Flights of Fancy) Ltd.
Paradise Works
Arden Forest Estate
Alcester
Warwickshire
B49 6EH
Tel. 01789 400077
www.blisscatalogue.co.uk
for various props

Brandon Marketing
Freepost DC741
PO Box 102
Doncaster
South Yorkshire
DN5 9BR
Tel. 01302 788138
www.brandonmarketing.co.uk
for bath resurfacing kit

Dulux Decorator Centres
Tel. 0161 9683000
for paint

Hewden Plant Hire
Tel. 0161 8488621

Hillarys Blinds Limited
Colwick Business Park
Private Rd. No. 2
Colwick
Nottingham, NG4 2JR
Tel. 0115 9617420
www.hillarys.co.uk
for blinds

Ideal-Standard
The Bathroom Works
National Avenue
Kingston-upon-Hull, HU5 4HS
Tel. 01482 346461
www.ideal-standard.co.uk

Satana
Unit E, Wyndford Industrial Estate
Higher Halstock Leigh
Yeovil
Somerset, BA22 9QX
Tel. 01935 891888
www.heatedmirrors-satana.uk.com
for heated mirror

Screwfix Direct
Tel. 0500 414141
www.screwfix.com
for tools & fixings

Shackerley (Holdings) Group Ltd
139 Wigan Road
Euxton
Chorley
Lancashire, PR7 6JJ
Tel. 01257 273114
www.shackerley.com
for glass block wall

Travis Perkins Trading Co. Limited
Tel. 01604 752424

Trevi Showers
The Bathroom Works
National Avenue
Kingston-upon-Hull
HU5 4HS
Tel. 01482 470788
www.trevishowers.co.uk

associations

National Home Improvement Council
Tel. 020 78288230

British Bathroom Council
Tel. 01782 747074

Builders Merchants Federation
Tel. 020 74391753
advice on building materials and lists of suppliers

Electrical Contractors Association
Tel. 020 73134800

Federation of Master Builders
Tel. 020 72427583

Health and Safety Executive
Tel. 0541 545500

Heating and Ventilating Contractors Association
Telephone number as for Electrical Contractors Association

Hire Association Europe
Tel. 0121 3777707
equipment hire

Institute of Plumbing
Tel. 01708 472791

Institution of Electrical Engineers
Tel. 020 72401871

Institution of Structural Engineers
Tel. 020 72354535

Royal Institute of British Architects
Tel. 020 75805533

the authors

Julian Cassell and Peter Parham have run their own building and decorating business for several years, having successfully renovated a variety of large and small scale properties around the UK. These award-winning authors have written a number of books covering all aspects of DIY, and their innovative approach has made them popular television and radio guests.

acknowledgements

We would like to thank the following individuals for supplying props, advice and general help throughout the production of this book – David House at Hewden Hire in Bruton, Andrew Toogood at Bradfords in Yeovil, Colin and Ros Lawrence, John White and Richard Hooper at B.J. White in Yeovil, Michael and Sue Read, and Bill Dove.

At Murdoch Books we would like to extend our gratitude to all those who have helped put this book together, but special thanks to Alastair Laing, Michelle Pickering and Iain MacGregor for dealing with all our problems with their customary ease.

Also, a big thank you to Tim Ridley for not only his expertise behind the camera, but also his contributions in front of it. Grazie mille to Marina Sala, his more than able assistant, and, as always, many thanks to Adele for her expertise in both the catering and consultation departments. The Publisher would like to give special thanks to Armitage Shanks, Ideal-Standard and Screwfix.

First published in 2001 by Murdoch Books UK Ltd
Copyright© 2001 Murdoch Books UK Ltd

ISBN 1 85391 953 5
A catalogue record for this book is available from the British Library.

All photography by Tim Ridley and copyright Murdoch Books UK Ltd except: p6 Ideal-Standard, p7 Armitage Shanks, p8 Fired Earth, pp10–11 Armitage Shanks, p15 Armitage Shanks (both), pp20–1 Armitage Shanks, p22 Armitage Shanks (both), p23 top and bottom right Armitage Shanks bottom left Ideal-Standard, p30 valves Ideal-Standard bottom right Armitage Shanks, p31 all pictures Ideal-Standard, p36–7 Armitage Shanks, p53 bottom right Armitage Shanks, p57 bottom right Ideal-Standard, p59 bottom right Ideal-Standard, p61 bottom right Armitage Shanks, pp64–5 Ideal-Standard, pp66–7 all pictures Ideal-Standard except p67 bottom right Armitage Shanks, pp78–9 Armstrong, p80 left Ideal-Standard right Armitage Shanks, p81 left Armitage Shanks, p87 bottom right Armitage Shanks, pp96–7 Ideal-Standard, p98 Armitage Shanks (both), p99 bottom left and right Armitage Shanks, pp112–3 Ideal-Standard, pp124–5 Armitage Shanks, p133 bottom right Murdoch Books®/Meredith.

Commissioning Editor: **Iain MacGregor**   Managing Editor: **Anna Osborn**
Series Editor: **Alastair Laing**   Design Manager: **Helen Taylor**
Project Editor: **Michelle Pickering**   Photo Librarian: **Bobbie Leah**
Designer: **Tim Brown**   Photographer: **Tim Ridley**
Design Concept: **Laura Cullen**   Illustrations: **Mike Badrocke**

CEO: **Robert Oerton**
Publisher: **Catie Ziller**
Production Manager: **Lucy Byrne**
International Sales Director: **Kevin Lagden**

Colour separation by Colourscan, Singapore
Printed in Singapore by Tien Wah Press

Murdoch Books UK Ltd
Ferry House, 51–57 Lacy Road, Putney
London, SW15 1PR, UK
Tel: +44 (0)20 8355 1480
Fax: +44 (0)20 8355 1499
Murdoch Books UK Ltd is a subsidiary of
Murdoch Magazines Pty Ltd.

UK Distribution
Macmillan Distribution Ltd
Houndsmills, Brunell Road
Basingstoke, Hampshire, RG1 6XS, UK
Tel: +44 (0) 1256 302 707
Fax: +44 (0) 1256 351 437
http://www.macmillan-mdl.co.uk

Murdoch Books®
GPO Box 1203
Sydney, NSW 1045, Australia
Tel: +61 (0)2 8220 2000
Fax: +61 (0)2 8220 2020
Murdoch Books® is a trademark of
Murdoch Magazines Pty Ltd.